MARK TWAIN'S LETTERS TO MARY

Mark Twain's Letters to Mary

EDITED WITH COMMENTARY BY LEWIS LEARY

10,462

NEW YORK AND LONDON

COLUMBIA UNIVERSITY PRESS

This collection of letters written to
a Friend of the Columbia Libraries
is dedicated to
The Friends of the Columbia Libraries

ACKNOWLEDGMENTS

THIS COLLECTION of letters, written by Mark Twain to Mary Benjamin Rogers and presented to the Columbia University Libraries by Mrs. Rogers in 1953, is printed now with permission of the Mark Twain Estate and the heirs of Mrs. Rogers. To provide background for incidents mentioned in the letters, newspaper and periodical accounts of Mark Twain's activities during those years have been quoted or paraphrased, and generous use has been made of accounts of his life by Albert Bigelow Paine, Clara Clemens, and Bernard De Voto. In addition, excerpts from correspondence with members of the Rogers family and with other friends have been woven into the narrative, and two of Mary Rogers's letters to her "Uncle Mark" and a telegram to him, which are among the Mark Twain Papers in the University of California Library, have been inserted in their proper place.

For permission to use these additional letters I am indebted to the Mark Twain Estate, the curators of the Mark Twain Papers at the University of California and of the Berg Collection in the New York Public Library, to Clifton Waller Barrett, and to Peter A. Salm. Other assistance has been given by Ruth Borel, Dallas Pratt, Mary Benjamin, Henry Rogers Benjamin, Mrs. Edgar Lackland, and Haven B.

Page. Marjorie Nicolson, Henry Nash Smith, Sheldon H. Harris, Sydney J. Kraus, Roland Baughman, Frederick Anderson, and John H. Waddell have all supplied essential points of information. The work put into collation of manuscripts and search for supporting information by my daughter, Carolyn Bartholet, would in a more just world entitle her to a place on the title page. No one has adventured toward publication by the Columbia University Press without incurring large debts to Miss Eugenia Porter, Dr. William Bridgwater, and, certainly, Mr. Henry Wiggins. In this instance, I am also indebted to Miss Joan McQuary who upholds their standards of excellence.

Columbia University   LEWIS LEARY
January, 1961

CONTENTS

ILLUSTRATIONS

MARK TWAIN'S LETTERS TO MARY

INTRODUCTION

AMONG the gifts of members of the Benjamin family to the Columbia University Libraries is the following series of letters written between 1900 and 1910 by Mark Twain to his young friend Mary Benjamin Rogers, the wife of Henry Huttleston Rogers, Jr.

Mrs. Rogers cherished these letters over many years. And other admirers of Mark Twain may well cherish them also. All but one of them were written during the last, lonely four years of his life, after the death of his wife, when his younger daughter was distressingly and incurably ill, and his older daughter was often away from home in pursuit of her musical career. He found partial substitute for them in young people like Mary Rogers, and made her one of his honorary nieces, and they had private jokes together at which his letters to her hint without quite revealing. They are not sad letters, whatever the undercurrent of dejection which occasionally moves through them. They reveal more than the pathos of an aging man who clings—though not, he was to admit, for more than a brief stretch at a time—to the quick vivacity of youth. Mark Twain could seldom be dull, even in his late despair. When his mood turned black or bitter, his words mocked it, so that even he must have smiled, as others smiled when he growled or grimaced, and as Mary Rogers must have smiled, fondly and with sympathy, as she read what he wrote to her.

Other collections of correspondence with others among the young friends of Mark Twain's later years might be put together, and they would reveal much which these letters to Mary Rogers reveal of tenderness and whimsy and ability to fit himself to the mood and expectations of his correspondent. Some were written to children and speak of games and secrets such as children love, of private understandings shared and intimate aspirations. Others were written seriously or half-humorously in admonition. What distinguishes the correspondence with Mary Rogers is that Mark Twain found in her a companion to whom he could express himself in many moods, sure of quick and sympathetic response.

After her Uncle Mark's death, Mary Benjamin Rogers lived a long, rich life, filled with satisfactions but also with sorrows. Both of her children predeceased her, and her last years might have been lonely had she not retained her vivacious interest in life, in other people, and in art. Her friends recall her late interest in painting, and many of them cherish her sketches in water color or oil, but they cherish more the memory of a person who was constantly and contagiously alive. As she went over these letters from Mark Twain some thirty years after they were written, she remembered "how amusing and stimulating and inspiring he was in that far flown day." She had become a grandmother by then, and Mark Twain had been long dead—"but," she wrote with confidence, "I shall see him again." She presented his letters to the Columbia Libraries in order that others might see him as she had seen him. They are printed now so that her wish can in part be realized.

1

A TRAVELER RETURNS

WHEN the steamship *Minnehaha* docked in New York on October 15, 1900, Samuel Clemens stepped ashore after a residence of nine years abroad. At the end of the next month he would be sixty-five. He had been ill, and he was happy to be home. Bankrupt five years before, he had circled the world on a triumphant lecture tour which paid his debts to the last penny. In every country people had crowded to hear Mark Twain drawl through laughter-crowded evenings of anecdote and wisdom. No American of his time was more intimately known or universally loved. Friends and reporters massed on the pier to give him a hero's welcome. Secretary of the Treasury Lyman J. Gage had sent orders that he be given freedom of the port. "Yes," Mark Twain told reporters, "I wrote to Secretary Gage, telling him that my baggage was in a 16,000 ton ship, which was quite enough to accommodate all I had, which while it consisted of a good many things, was not good enough to pay duty on, yet too good to throw away. I accordingly suggested that he write the customs people to let me in, as I thought they would be more likely to take his word than mine."

He talked on expansively, if not always with complete accuracy, about his travels. "I left America," he told them, "on

June 6, 1891, and went to Aix-les-Bains, France, where I spent the fall and winter. After that I went to Berlin, where I lectured, giving readings from my works. After this my next stop was the Riviera, where I remained for three months, going from there to the baths near Frankfurt, where I remained during the cholera season. Most of 1892 I spent in Florence where I rented a house. While there I wrote *Joan of Arc* and finished *Pudd'nhead Wilson*. For the next two years I was in France. I can't speak French yet."

He reminded them that in the spring of 1895 he had returned briefly to the United States to endure the worrisome and embarrassing business of meeting with creditors, almost a hundred of them, and that on July 15 of that year he had left New York for Cleveland to begin his grand tour, crossing the continent to the Pacific coast, lecturing, he remembered with a shudder, every night. Major J. B. Pond, who had accompanied him across the country as his agent, recalled the opening in Cleveland. "The great Music Hall there," he said, "gave him a splendid send-off with an audience of over 3,000 people who packed the building on a mid-July day, with the mercury in the nineties. He had been very ill, subject to many annoyances from being dragged from a sick bed to appear in supplementary [bankruptcy] proceedings in New York the day before starting, and suffering from a huge carbuncle that had kept him confined in his house for seven weeks."

Readers of *Following the Equator* in which Mark Twain in 1897 had told of his adventures, remembered that carbuncle: "The dictionary," he had said then, "says a carbuncle is a kind of jewel. Humor is out of place in a dictionary."

"From Cleveland," continued Major Pond, "he went by steamers *Northland* and *Northwest* to Duluth, Minnesota, and St. Paul and Winnipeg, and over the Great Northern route to Puget Sound, Vancouver, and Victoria, British Columbia, where he sailed on the 21st day of August by steamship *Warrimoo* for Australia, having delivered twenty-four lectures in twenty-four cities. . . . He gave himself four years to make enough money to pay his debts. Two years from that time," said the Major, "he wrote me from Lucerne, Switzerland, that he was now satisfied that those debts would be paid off a year earlier than the prophecy and without further help from the platform, and that he was now a cheerful man."

Mark Twain rambled on, providing a good show and, as usual, excellent copy. He spoke of Sydney, "where I lectured or, more properly speaking, gave readings from my works to the English-speaking people. I also visited Tasmania and New Zealand. . . . I then proceeded to India, lecturing in Ceylon, Bombay, and Calcutta. I then sailed for South Africa, arriving at Delagoa Bay in April, 1896. In South Africa I visited Kimberley, Johannesburg, and finally Cape Town. I met Oom Paul. I had heard and read all about him—hat, beard, frock coat, pipe, and everything else. The picture is a true likeness. At this time the Jameson raiders were in jail, and I visited them and made a little speech trying to console them. I told them of the advantages of being in jail. 'This jail is as good as any other,' I said, 'and besides being in jail has its advantages. A lot of great men had been in jail. If Bunyan had not been in jail, he would never have written *Pilgrim's Progress*. And then jail is responsible for *Don Quixote*, so you see, being in jail is not so bad after all.' Finally I told them that they ought to remember that many great men had been compelled to go through life without ever having the advantage of having been in jail.

Some of the prisoners didn't seem to take much to the joke, while others seemed much amused.

"All this time my family was with me, and after a short trip to Cape Town we took a steamer for Southampton. On arriving in England we went to Guilford, where I took a furnished house, remaining two months, after which for ten months our home was in London." He liked it there, especially the place just outside of the city which they had just left, the farmhouse at Dollis Hill, forty minutes by carriage from Piccadilly, of which he had written enthusiastically to friends in New York: "Mrs. Clemens has got herself reconciled to housekeeping, the servants are first rate, and things are going smoothly. There are six acres of hay and sheep, the lawn is spacious and there are plenty of old forest trees for shade." All this time, he told the reporters, "I was lecturing, reading, or working hard in other ways, writing magazine stories and doing other literary work.

"After London came Vienna, to which city we went in in September, 1898, remaining until May of the following year, in order to allow my daughters to take music lessons from a man who spelled his name Leschetizky. He had plenty of identification, you see, and with all that seemed to be a pretty smart fellow. After Vienna, where, by the way, I had lots of fun watching the Reichsrath, we returned to London, in which city and in Sweden we have been until our departure for home some days ago, and now I am home again and you have got the history of a considerable part of my life."

This was the Mark Twain people loved best, jovially discursive, with a twinkle in his eye and a sly sting to his words. What he did not tell them was the devastating shock of the death of his daughter Susy two years before, the distressing and then incurable illness which had been discovered in his youngest daughter Jean, and the increasing invalidism of his wife who seemed never to recover from the shock of Susy's death. If the reporters knew of these things, they retained enough of nineteenth-century grace to refrain from asking about them. But they peppered him with other questions.

"How about your plans?" he was asked.

"I am absolutely unable to speak of my plans," he replied, "inasmuch as I have none, and I do not expect to lecture." That last negative was emphasized and seconded by Major Pond: "I wrote offering him $10,000 if he would deliver ten lectures on his return," said the Major. "He replied that no terms I could offer would remove his prejudice from the platform."

Questions then inevitably turned to the political battle which raged between Republican President William McKinley and the fiery, silver-tongued Democrat William Jennings Bryan who was trying for a second time to defeat him and who was due in New York the next day to bring his Eastern campaign to a close with speeches at Madison Square and Cooper Union. "How are you on expansion?" Mark Twain was asked. "Are you with the President or with those that style themselves anti-imperialists?"

"Yes," he answered, "as near as I can find out, I think that I am an anti-imperialist. I was not, though, until some time ago, for when I first heard of the acquisition of the present Pacific possessions I thought it a good thing for a country like America to release those people from bondage of suffering and oppression that has lasted 300 years, but when I read the Paris treaty I changed my mind."

"You are going to vote for Mr. Bryan, then, are you?"

"No, I am a Mugwump. I don't know who I am going to

vote for. I must look over the field. Then, you know, I have been out of the country for a long time, and I might not be allowed to register."

"You are still a citizen of the United States, are you not?"

"Well, I guess I am. I've been paying taxes on this side for the last nine years. I believe, though, a man can run for President without a vote, can't he? If this is so, then, I am a candidate for President."

No one took him seriously, but every reporter must have scratched the jocose declaration onto his pad. And that reminded someone that newspapers had reported Mark Twain at work on an autobiography so revelatory of his honest opinion of people and events that it was not to be published for one hundred years.

"It is true I am writing it," he said.

"That's not a joke is it?"

"No, I said. it seriously, that's why they take it as a joke. You know, I never told the truth in my life that someone didn't say I was lying, while, on the other hand, I never told a lie that someone didn't take it as fact."

"Well, it's not wrong, anyway, to tell a lie sometimes, is it?"

"That's right, exactly right. If you can disseminate facts by telling the truth, why that's the way to do it, and if you can't except by doing a little lying, well, that's right, too, isn't it? I do it."

But time was getting on and Mark Twain "had become restless, . . . and the many friends surrounding him on the pier managed to rescue him from the clutches of the newspapermen, who had been firing questions at him since he first arrived."

"I'll see you again," he said. "I'll be at the Earlingham all winter. I am not going to Hartford till next year."

Then, reported the New York *Times*, "with a pleasant nod of the head the famous writer, accompanied by his friends, began a search for his baggage."

Among those who welcomed him back to New York was the family of Henry Huttleston Rogers, one of the founders and for many years active in the management of the Standard Oil Company, whom Mark Twain thought of as "my closest and most valuable friend." Rogers had come to his assistance seven years before, to straighten the snarl of Clemens's business affairs. He had placated creditors and made possible the triumphant financial recuperation which Mark Twain now celebrated. Rogers was not only acute in business; he was a good companion on every occasion, at a boxing match, a horse show, the opera, at billiards, or just for an evening of talk. He was self-made, like Mark Twain, and wonderfully successful, so that he seemed everything a man should be: "young in spirit, and in looks, complexion, and bearing, easy and graceful in his movements, kindhearted, attractive, winning, a natural gentleman, the best bred gentleman," Mark Twain thought, "I have met on either side of the ocean."

He was equally fond of the Rogers family, especially of the first Mrs. Rogers who had died while he was abroad, who was gracious as a hostess and quietly kind as a friend. "She had such a gift for making me feel welcome," he said, and she always remembered to have a glass of milk put at Mark Twain's place at the table. She was one of the most generous women he had known, and he had been proud, he said, to have been asked by her to speak at the ceremonies which dedicated the library which she and her husband had donated in their children's names some years before to Mr. Rogers's birthplace, the village of Fairhaven in Massachusetts.

He did not yet know the second Mrs. Rogers quite so well, though she had visited the Clemenses in Europe, and was to become a valued and beloved friend.

Henry Rogers's eldest daughter, Anne, was married to William Evarts Benjamin, a bookdealer and publisher, who had provided welcome cash which helped stave off some of Mark Twain's more persistent creditors when he purchased rights to the multi-volumed *Library of American Literature* which had been held by the author's bankrupt publishing firm. Urban Broughton, husband of the second daughter, Clara, worked with his father-in-law in investigating the practicability of the type-setting machine on the development of which Mark Twain had invested and lost so much. Mai, the youngest daughter, had stopped over briefly with the Clemenses in London a few months before their return to the United States.

But it was Henry Rogers's youngest child, his son and namesake, who was Mark Twain's favorite. He was a lively, affectionate boy, so bounding with energy that his Uncle Mark called him the "Electric Spark" or the "Prince of Activity." Three years before Mark Twain had dedicated *Following the Equator* affectionately "to my young friend Harry Rogers, with recognition of what he is, and apprehension of what he may become unless he form himself a little more closely on the model of the Author." Formerly a young playmate, a schoolboy at the Berkeley and Browning schools in New York, and a quick and willing pupil to his Uncle Mark in learning the delicate mysteries of billiards, Harry was now almost twenty-one and a junior at Columbia College, and he had recently announced his engagement to nineteen-year-old Mary Benjamin, a niece by marriage of his eldest sister.

Mary Benjamin was descended from another of New

York's most respected families. Her grandfather had been Parke Benjamin, editor and man of letters, long associated with such people as William Cullen Bryant in civic and literary activities. As a young man he had been part of the circle in Boston which centered about his Harvard classmate Oliver Wendell Holmes. In New York he had been a literary advisor to Horace Greeley, had befriended Edgar Allan Poe, corresponded with Henry Wadsworth Longfellow, and given early recognition to the sketches of Nathaniel Hawthorne. His second son, Mary's father, was George Hilliard Benjamin, who was also a remarkable man, educated at Union College in Schenectady, then in France and Germany, with a Ph.D. from the University of Freiburg. For nine years he had practiced medicine in Albany, where his daughter was born, but for the past sixteen years had been prominently successful in New York as a patent attorney. Well born and cultured, with something more than an amateur's talent for painting, Mary Benjamin had auburn hair much the color that Mark Twain's had once been, and she had a sense of humor which responded to his.

Five days after his arrival in New York Mark Twain was called hurriedly to Hartford by the death of his old friend and literary colleague, Charles Dudley Warner. Mrs. Clemens was not well enough to accompany him, so his daughter Clara went in her place. After the funeral they looked together into the house which Mark Twain had built in Hartford. It was filled with memories of happy family times extending over almost twenty years before the flight to Europe. But now they could only remember that this was the house in which Susy had died alone while they were away. Only a few months before, Mark Twain had written Henry Rogers from London: "It looks now as if we shall go to Hartford, but we can't make up our minds. Half of our friends there are dead, and we sort of shudder at the prospect." Now, having seen the old house again, he knew certainly, he said, "that if we ever enter the old house again our hearts will break."

Returning to New York, he wrote what seems to be his first letter to Mary Benjamin, addressing her in much the playful tone he had used in dedicating his last book of travels to young Harry:

New York
October 25, 1900

Dear Miss Benjamin:

I feel a deep personal interest in this fortunate marriage because I helped to rear Harry Rogers and make him what he is. I gave him the high moral touch which you will discover in him in spots. In order to testify to you how thankful I am to you for taking him off my hands, I had the idea of sending you a diamond coronet as a bridal present, but I gave it up because I was not able to find any fresh diamonds of this year's crop, they are all of earlier vintages, and some were second-hand; and so I have finally decided to ask you to accept a set of my books instead; and this is all the better anyway, for diamonds invite the burglar, but he will not take the books, except by request.

Hoping you two will have a long and happy life and great prosperity—a wish in which Mrs. Clemens joins me—I am

Sincerely yours,

S. L. Clemens

At the end of the next week, on November 7, the Benjamin residence at 46 East 74th Street was decorated with palms and chrysanthemums for the marriage ceremony performed that afternoon by the Reverend E. Walpole Warren, rector of St. James's. The bride was gowned in white crepe de Chine, trimmed with chiffon and lace, and she wore a collar of diamonds and pearls given her by the bridegroom's father, and a diamond pendant, the gift of the bridegroom. Three days later the young couple sailed on the *Kaiser Wilhelm II* for Gibraltar, Naples, and Genoa, on a wedding trip which was planned to keep them abroad for a year.

THE DEAN OF AMERICAN HUMOR

MEANWHILE Mark Twain was caught up by wave after wave of ceremonious public and private greeting. He and his family moved into a handsomely furnished residence at 14 West Tenth Street. Engagements piled up, sometimes as many as four or five a week. Magazines and lecture agents sought him out. "The telephone rang so steadily," said his daughter Clara, "that the butler got no time for his work." She could find no words to describe "the atmosphere of adulation that swept across this threshold. Every day was like a great festive occasion. We felt that a large party was going on and that by and by the guests would be leaving. But there was no leaving. More and more came."

Mark Twain's calendar was so filled that he sometimes had difficulty keeping up with it. The Lotus Club, for example, planned a dinner for him on November 10, at which men of reputation in business, literature, and politics would meet to honor the "Dean of American Humor." Henry Rogers was there, Senator Chauncey Depew, William Dean Howells, Thomas Bailey Aldrich, Booker T. Washington, John Kendrick Bangs, and many more. But as time approached for the banquet to begin, the guest of honor did not arrive. A messenger was sent to fetch him. Mark Twain met him di-

sheveled at the door. "I am sorry," he said, "but I had forgotten this was Saturday; I thought it was Friday; I'll go right
upstairs and dress. It won't take me fifteen minutes." As a
result, it was ten o'clock before the after-dinner talking began,
and it went on for hours as Mr. Depew, Mr. Bangs, and Mr.
Howells joined others in convincing their guest that he had
returned to "the house of friends." "Sinners love him," said
St. Clair McKelway, "and saints are content to wait for
him." When Mark Twain rose to speak, he was cheered
"long and heartily" before, "pushing his bushy white hair
from his forehead," he began his characteristic drawling remarks.

At affairs of this kind, he usually spoke briefly, in broad
good humor, often quizzically personal in a manner such as
only he could carry off. When the New York Press Club held
a reception for him on November 12, "there gathered together," reported the New York *Times*, "such a crowd as
the newspapermen had never had in their clubrooms before." Colonel William L. Brown, president of the club,
opened the ceremonies by pretending with straight-faced
sobriety that, though he had never read a word Mark Twain
had written, he honored him and welcomed him because of
his multitude of praiseworthy personal virtues, which he
proceeded to detail at fulsome length. The humorist at once
rose to respond:

"Gentlemen," he said, "your Chairman has presented me
with compliments. I have often said that I felt like using a
gun on anyone who treated me that way, but as I haven't a
gun, I'll just give the Chairman a dose of his own medicine.
I ask you to look at him. You behold an old, old man. His
features will deceive you. Apparently he is a person hardened
to everything, a man dead to all honest impulse, one who

has committed all kinds of crimes. And yet these features belie themselves. Instead of leading a life of wickedness, he began in a Sunday School, and will end there. This man really has all the known virtues, but he practises them secretly. Gentlemen, you know him too well for me to further prolong this introduction."

Mark Twain then took his seat, "while the audience in an uproar of laughter, looked at Colonel Brown to see if he would successfully turn aside the joke on him. The Colonel did very well, simply saying that he had not known before that his friend, Mark Twain, was such a good judge of character." Other speakers spoke expansively also of the virtues of their guest. "I don't mind the slanders," Mark Twain reminded them. "The facts are what I object to. I don't want any of my true history getting abroad." He appealed to them as fellow journalists to keep it from the public. When Commissioner of Charities John W. Keller made it plain in his speech that he had read everything Mark had written, the humorist beamed with pretended great pride. "There was a man here tonight," he remarked, "that said he had never read any of my books. That hurts me. And he seemed to be intelligent, too. But he was not. Mr. Keller is an intelligent man. He said he had read all my books. He fairly oozes intelligence."

Three nights later when the Society of American Authors gave a dinner at Delmonico's in his honor, Mark Twain referred to the incident again. Once more he was introduced with affectionate praise. "It seems to me a most difficult thing," he drawled in response, "for any man, no matter how well prepared, to say anything about me that is not complimentary. Sometimes I am almost persuaded that I am what the Chairman says I am. As a rule the Chairman begins

by saying something to my discredit, and he feels that he is
clear off the track and that he is really not telling the truth,
and then he begins to compliment me. Nothing bites so
deep down as the facts of a man's life. The real life that you
live is a life of interior sin. Everyone believes I am just a
monument of all the virtues. Someday there will be a Chairman who will be able to give the true side of my character.
I thought I had met such a Chairman the other night at the
Press Club, but when he said he had never read any of my
books I knew he was a liar."

And so, lightly, half-serious, half-gay, but a showman on
every occasion, Mark Twain became a center of admiring
attention in New York. Sometimes when the hour grew late,
he pled exhaustion: "I shall have to leave you. I am old."
"No! No!", the company would cry. But he persisted, firmly,
humorously: "I am a respectable fellow now," he protested.
"I wasn't once upon a time. Now I must protect my good
name." Every exit was made with a quip, but with every exit
he was more tired. "I declined seven banquets yesterday," he
wrote late in December to a friend in England. Friends in
New York worried about him. "If he had eaten all the dinners
proposed," said Albert Bigelow Paine, "he would not have
lived to enjoy his public honors a month. As it was, he accepted more dinners than he could eat, and presently fell to
the habit of arriving when the banquet was about over and
the after-dinner speaking about to begin." But even so, the
strain told on him: he looked drawn and was increasingly
plagued with a hacking cough.

He spoke that winter before the Public Education Associa-
tion, at the Aldine Association dinner, and the Saint Nicholas
Association banquet; he talked of "The Disappearance of
Literature" at the Nineteenth Century Club, of the in-

iquitousness of foreign occupation of Cuba at the Berkeley Lyceum, and of the necessity for municipal reform at the City Club; he introduced Winston Churchill to a gathering at the Waldorf, and Henry Watterson at the Lincoln's birthday celebration at Carnegie Hall. As the year drew to a close, he composed "A Greeting from the Nineteenth to the Twentieth Century," in which the old speaks in this manner to the new: "I bring you the stately nation named Christendom, returning bedraggled, besmirched, and dishonored from pirate raids on Kiao-Chou, Manchuria, South Africa, and the Philippines, with her soul full of meanness, her pocket full of boodle, and her mouth full of pious hypocrisies. Give her soap and a towel, but hide the mirror." In February he contributed "To the Person Sitting in Darkness" to the *North American Review* in scornful attack on what he considered the dubious morality of missionaries. "It always puzzled me," said his daughter, "how Mark Twain could manage to have an opinion on every incident, accident, invention, or disease in the world."

Clearly a man of his age and explosive attitudes could not keep up this pace. The Clemenses spent the summer of 1901 at Saranac Lake, in a log cabin "just large enough," said Clara, "for the family and no more." In August, Mark Twain joined Henry Rogers on his yacht *Kanawha* for a cruise along the Maine coast. He had an hilariously good time, especially with young Harry Rogers, recently returned from his honeymoon. "Mr. Clemens and Harry have attracted," he said, "a good deal of attention, and men have expressed a resolve to turn over a new leaf and copy after them from this time out." At Bath, a friend came aboard "to pay his respects," said Mark Twain, "to Harry and Mr. Clemens, he having heard of their reputation from the clergy of these coasts."

He was invited by the whole company to join them at poker, "apparently as a courtesy and in a spirit of seeming hospitality. . . . Mr. Rogers lent him clothes to go home in."

Mark Twain resented the onrush of age, and delighted in the kind of irresponsibility which such a cruise allowed. "The whole scheme of things is turned wrong end to," he said. "Life should begin with age and its privileges and accumulations, and end with youth and its capacity to splendidly enjoy such advantages." Young people had "capacity to enjoy without the chance"; people as old and rheumatic as he had "the chance without the capacity." But Mark Twain still thought of himself as young, and liked youngness around him. It was secret to no one that his wife affectionately referred to him as Youth.

That fall the Clemenses returned, not to New York, but to a rented house just outside the city, in Riverdale. During the winter Mark Twain worked strenuously for municipal reform in a campaign directed against Croker and Tammany Hall. He and Howells were given honorary doctorates at Yale, he delivered the Founders' Day Address at the Players Club, attended the mayor's dinner in honor of Prince Henry of Prussia, and nipped in the bud a movement to name a political reform party the Mark Twain Party.

He was overwhelmed with letters from people who liked his books or his political ideas. He was most fond of those from young people, particularly young girls, and he formed his correspondents into a Juggernaut Club, to be made up of one member only from each country, "and there can be no male member but myself . . . for I do not represent a country . . . but am merely member-at-large for the human race." These girls were his nieces, he said, and he was proud of them: "one . . . is a princess of a royal house, another is the daughter of a village bookseller . . . for the only qualification for membership is intellect and the spirit of good will; other distinctions, hereditary or acquired, do not count."

Early in April he joined Henry Rogers on a cruise through the West Indies, for another interlude of relaxation and draw-poker. While he was away, Mrs. Clemens bought a house in Tarrytown into which the family planned to move in the fall. But when Mark Twain returned to Riverdale in May, after a visit to Missouri where he had steamboated on the Mississippi again with his old pilot friend Horace Bixby, he found Mrs. Clemens disturbingly and seriously ill. Henry Rogers brought the *Kanawha* up the Hudson to Riverdale so that she could be taken with least possible tax on her strength to York Harbor in Maine where it was hoped the change of air might help her back to health. Early in August, however, she became alarmingly worse. Henry Rogers kept his yacht ready, said Clemens, "to fly here, and take us to Riverdale on telegraphic notice." By October her condition was so serious that he doubted whether they could get her back to Riverdale at all: "We could not venture transportation by Mr. Rogers's yacht. She would not be able to endure the sea effect."

Instead, he went to Boston to arrange for passage by rail directly from York Harbor to Riverdale in a special car. He stormed at delays, indignant that anyone he loved so well should suffer: self-accusing, frustrated and helpless, he was completely miserable. That winter the Riverdale house was hushed by nurses. Young Jean was desperately ill with pneumonia, and her sister Clara was worn beyond her strength in caring for their mother. Clemens was allowed to see his wife only briefly, a few minutes a day, sometimes not at all for weeks at a time. He wrote little notes to her daily, and he signed them Youth, but he did not feel young at all. Ironically when Harper's arranged a sixty-seventh birthday dinner for Mark Twain, the celebration was held on his wife's birthday, on November 27, 1902, rather than on his which fell three days later but on a Sunday. After speeches spoken then in his honor, Mark Twain began his response by explaining, "A part of me is not present; the larger part, the better part, is yonder at her home, and . . . although she is going to be confined to her bed for many months . . . she is coming along very well."

But Mark Twain was too optimistic, for his wife did not recover. He occupied himself as best he could, at writing, at reading, but he was restless and he suffered himself that winter from bronchitis, and from his sickbed wrote Brander Matthews a long letter about his attempts to read the novels of Walter Scott, a letter so petulantly but humorously and acutely critical that Matthews preserved it carefully as one of the brightest among the papers which would be contributed in his name to the Columbia University Library. In May, Clemens was cheered to learn that a Mark Twain Association had been established in his native Missouri and that a Mark Twain Day would be celebrated at the forthcoming St. Louis Fair.

Even in semi-retirement he continued to receive public notice. So vehement had been his crusades against political abuses and so compelling his arguments for reform that one newspaper suggested that as "our ablest and most conspicuous private citizen," he be drafted at once for public office, even the Presidency: he was "the greatest man of his day in private life, and entitled to the fullest measure of recognition." But Mark Twain would have none of this.

Early that summer he watched from the deck of Henry Rogers's yacht while Sir Thomas Lipton's brave *Shamrock* tried in vain to win the American Cup from Commodore Vanderbilt's sturdy *Reliance*, and he made light-hearted quips about the race to newspapermen. But he did not feel light-hearted. "Man," he said, "was made at the end of a week's work, when God was tired."

In July, 1903, Henry Rogers took the Clemenses in the *Kanawha* from Riverdale to the Lackawanna pier, where they boarded a train which would take them on a last visit to Mrs. Clemens's girlhood home in Elmira. There they spent the summer, quietly and sadly amid scenes which had once served as background for happier times. Here Mark Twain had written happily on *The Adventures of Huckleberry Finn* and *A Connecticut Yankee in King Arthur's Court*, but that had been years ago, and he did no writing now. Early in October he placed flowers on his daughter Susy's grave, probably, he thought, for the last time. The next day he and his wife returned to New York to sail on the *Princess Irene* for Italy, where a villa had been rented for them below Fiesole, near Florence. All ties were being cut, for "he did not look forward to returning," but "expected," said his friend Howells, to live in Florence always, because of Mrs. Clemens's health but also "because he can't stand the nervous storms and stresses here. He takes things intensely hard, and America is too much for him."

The last days before sailing were busily filled. Henry Rogers saw to the drawing up of a contract with Harper's which gave that publishing firm first rights to everything which Mark Twain had written or would write, and which guaranteed him a substantial income for life. Frequent hurried trips on the *Kanawha* to the Rogers summer home at

Fairhaven were necessary for the arrangement of final details. Harper's arranged an elaborate farewell dinner. Mrs. Rogers filled the Clemens cabin with flowers and fruit.

In Florence, Mrs. Clemens lingered for months, now well, now worse. Early in April, Clara made her debut there as a concert singer, astonishing everyone "including me," said her father, "with the richness and volume of her voice, and with her trained ability to handle it." Her mother roused briefly in affectionate response to Clara's success, but the next day she was desperately ill again. Mark Twain filled lonely, reminiscent hours with work on his autobiography or in sitting for a portrait which was to be exhibited at the St. Louis Fair and wondering whether Mrs. Clemens would like it. He looked for a villa near Florence where they could settle permanently, and on June 4, 1904, took an option on two so that his wife could choose between them. But on the next evening, which was Sunday, she died, "after twenty-two months," her husband wrote, "of unjust and unearned suffering."

He wrote at once to Henry Rogers: "My head is stunned and muddled. I cannot think clearly. Clara is prostrate, ever since Sunday night, and seldom speaks, seldom eats anything." Mark Twain was bewildered and lost. "Death came in an instant," he said. "No one was dreaming of danger. Mrs. Clemens was chatting cheerfully a moment before."

3

"THE BELLE OF NEW YORK"

so in the summer of 1904 Mark Twain returned another time to the United States where he had not thought to live again. Mrs. Clemens was put to rest beside Susy in Elmira. Mark Twain and his two daughters retired to the quiet of the Berkshires. Clara, prostrated still, was under the charge of a trained nurse. Jean, who sought strenuous therapy out of doors, was seriously hurt when thrown while riding a horse. Their father did little or nothing, except grieve in loneliness. When cool weather set in, they returned to New York, to a house at 21 Fifth Avenue, on the corner of Ninth Street. When Henry Rogers returned in September on the White Star Steamship *Oceanic* after seven weeks abroad, at Vichy in France, where he had taken his wife because of her ill health, Mark Twain was among those on the pier to greet him.

That winter he worked lovingly over the conception of a fanciful story to be called *Eve's Diary*, which would convey, he hoped, something of his reverent devotion to the spirit of gentle womanliness which he had known so clearly in his wife. He was desperately alone. Clara spent many months at a rest home in Norfolk. Jean needed an attendant with her at all times. For the rest of his life Mark Twain was to be lonely. He sought companionship, especially young companionship which in its innocence and vigor recalled happier days.

During the summer of 1905 he rented a house at Lone Tree Hill in Dublin, New Hampshire. His neighbors there included Thomas Wentworth Higginson, Franklin Mac-Veagh, Raphael Pumpelly of Harvard, former Secretary of the Interior Ethan A. Hitchcock, and Abbott Thayer, whose wife Mark Twain had first known when she was a girl forty years before and had been one of the "pilgrims" who had traveled abroad with him as he collected materials for *Innocents Abroad.* But there were young people there also. "Paint, literature, science, statesmanship, history, professorship, law, morals—these are all represented here," said Mark Twain, in better spirits now, "yet crime is substantially unknown." He liked Dublin, the view of Monadnock, the company, the stimulation to work again. "We were fortunate to find this place," he told Henry Rogers. "It is perfectly satisfactory. Jean is outdoors all the time; I am indoors all the time, and both of us are content. Clara has lost some of her voice again—thinks the cause is bronchial. But she says she is having a delightful time, and drives out every day, over our pretty country roads."

For the first time in years Mark Twain was able to keep steadily, uninterruptedly at work. "I am ashamed to say," he confessed, "what an intolerable pile of manuscript I ground out." He puttered over a long book which he planned to call "Twenty Thousand Years Among the Microbes," supposed to be written "by a Microbe" and "Translated out of the original Microbic by Mark Twain." He wrote enthusiastically, and then put the manuscript away to finish the next summer. But, like many things which he began during these lonely years, it was never completed. He worked also over *The Mysterious Stranger* and further on *What Is Man?*, his "wicked" books over which he had been puttering at odd moments for several years. He completed *Eve's Diary* and sent it off to Harper's for publication, and he wrote his anti-vivisection story called "A Horse's Tale," which was also sadly nostalgic because his daughter Susy kept coming to his mind as he wrote of its gentle heroine. Early in October, he wrote Henry Rogers, "I have finished the fifth and last revising of 'A Horse's Tale' and am going to bed and stay there two weeks, for I am a free person once more."

Back in New York again for the winter, Mark Twain found himself again a public figure. Harper's gave him a tremendous seventieth birthday dinner on November 30, a "sky-scraping banquet," his friend Howells called it, at which "172 immortals sat down to the best Delmonico's could do, and remained glutting and guzzling food for reflection for five hours after the dinner was ended." Mark Twain's speech, thought Howells, "was divinely droll, sweet, touching, and wise." Some twenty tables were arranged in the banquet hall. In the head tier, Andrew Carnegie presided over one at Mark Twain's right, Colonel George Harvey of Harper's over one at his left, and William Dean Howells over another at the far flank. At Mark Twain's table sat such old friends as Henry Mills Alden, long editor of *Harper's Magazine*, the Reverend Joseph Twichell from Hartford, and Henry Rogers.

Through the early months of 1906 Mark Twain was called on to speak on several impressive occasions. The Society of American Illustrators had given him another birthday dinner, and he appeared with Sarah Bernhardt at a mass meeting to appeal for support of freedom-seeking revolutionaries in Russia. In January, he joined Booker T. Washington in an appeal for support of the Tuskegee Institute. In February, he spoke at a Dickens dinner and before the Ends of the Earth Club. In March, the doors of the Majestic Theater, where he was to address the West Side Young Men's Christian Association, were so jammed with people that newspapers the next day ran headlines to report "10,000 Stampeded at the Mark Twain Meeting." "His sound, breezy Mississippi Valley Americanism," said the New York *Mail*, "is a corrective to all sorts of snobbery."

But he liked best his talks before young audiences, especially to young female audiences. "Girls are charming creatures," he said. "I shall have to be twice seventy years old before I change my mind as to that." He rode uptown on the afternoon of March 7 to speak informally to the students of Barnard College, which he described as "the sex's annex to Columbia University." He was guest of the Barnard Union, a new organization which had been having trouble in enlisting members because its meetings had been open to all students so that girls who were asked to join the Union declined, with the explanation that they already enjoyed all its privileges. Mark Twain's popular presence made it possible now to demonstrate that "the Union, not being an all-inclusive body, has the right to keep certain privileges for its members alone." Therefore it announced in the *Barnard Bulletin* that attendance would be limited: "two tickets for the Mark Twain lecture to be given to each member of the Union who has paid her dues and one ticket to each Freshman."

Mark Twain began his rambling remarks, reported the *Bulletin*, by saying that "he had nothing to talk about, but he did have some fine illustrations he was going to get in somehow. 'The Caprice of Memory,' he thought would be

a good subject, though he might just as well talk of morals.
For it is better to teach than to practice them; better to
confer morals on others than to experiment too much with
them one's self. As to his first illustration, Mr. Clemens
told how he had once had in his possession a watermelon—
a Missouri watermelon, and therefore large and luscious.
Most people would have said he had stolen it. But the word
'steal' was too much for him, a good boy; in fact the best
boy in town. He said he had *extracted* it from a grocer's cart,
for 'extract' refers to dentistry, and more accurately expresses
how he got that melon; since as the dentist never extracts his
own teeth, so it wasn't his own melon. But the melon was
green, and because it was so, Mark Twain began to reflect.
And reflection is the beginning of morality. It was his duty
to take it back and admonish that grocer of the evil of selling
green melons. The moral, Mr. Clemens said, was that the
grocer repented of his sins and soon was perched on the high-
est pinnacle of virtue."

He closed what he later called his "moral sermon to the
Barnard girls" with another illustration: "Mark Twain said
that in his family there had been a prejudice against going
fishing unless you asked permission, and it was bad judgment to ask permission." The girls were entranced and breath-
less with laughter. "After his address, Mr. Clemens received
the members of the Union and their friends in the alcove
near the Trustees' room, where lemonade and small cakes
added to the interest of the discussion."

Not many weeks later, on April 2, he spoke to the Vassar
alumnae—"all Vassar, ancient and modern," he said, "packed
itself into the Hudson Theater, and I was there." After the
talk, "I held a reception on the stage for an hour or two,"
and "I was hoping," he confessed, "somebody would want

to kiss me for my mother, but didn't dare suggest it myself."
But then one of them did, and "I did what I could to make
it contagious, and succeeded." It required, he explained,
some art on his part, particularly in seeming to enjoy the
attention of the older girls as much as the younger, "without
discrimination, but I averaged the percentage to my advantage, and without anybody's suspecting it."

The next night he was guest of honor at a reception given
by the Women's University Club, at which, reported the
newspapers, "five hundred women shook hands with him and
showered him with pretty speeches." He found almost all
of them "young and lovely, untouched by care, unfaded by
age." Barnard girls were there, old friends whom he had met
before, and girls from Vassar, Smith, Wellesley, and Rad-
cliffe, with "a sprinkling of college girls from the South, from
the Middle West and the Pacific coast," even two girls who
were granddaughters of "fellow passengers who sailed with
me," he said, "on the *Quaker City* in the *Innocents Abroad*
excursion thirty-nine years before." They made Mark Twain
feel old and benign and avuncular, and they charmed him
completely. "One sweet creature wanted to whisper in my
ear, and I was nothing loath. She raised her dainty form on
tiptoe, lifting herself with a grip of her velvet hands on my
shoulders, and put her lips to my ear and said, 'How do you
like being the belle of New York?'" Mark Twain pretended,
he said, to be crimsoned with blushes, but—"It was so . . .
satisfying."

Three days later he attended the annual luncheon of the
Smith College Club of New York. "I should like to be
elected the belle of New York," he confessed to them, "so
that I could come to these luncheons all the time." His
charm was effective: the girls by acclamation invited him

to be annually thereafter a guest at their reunion meetings.

During April, he also presided over a meeting held by the Association of the Blind at the Waldorf Astoria, and he appeared with Maxim Gorky at a dinner given at the Club A House on lower Fifth Avenue. With Howells, Peter Finley Dunne, Jane Addams, and others, he became an active member of the American Auxiliary Movement to Aid the Cause of Freedom in Russia. He accepted place on a committee to purchase arms to aid Gorky in his revolutionary movement. When scoffers asked, "Why should this country assist . . . the Russian people in their revolutionary movements?" Mark Twain answered: "Because we were quite willing to accept France's assistance when we were in the throes of our Revolution, and we have always been grateful for that assistance. It is our turn now to pay that debt of gratitude by helping another oppressed people in its struggle for liberty, and we must either do it or confess that our gratitude to France was only eloquent words, with no sincerity back of it."

Enthusiasm for Gorky's cause was dampened when newspapers revealed that the woman with whom the Russian writer lived was not, according to American standards, his wife. One New York hotel after another turned the couple out, and public opinion—a delicate fabric, said Mark Twain, "which shrivels like the webs of morning at the slightest touch"—turned against the movement to aid a foreign revolution. "Gorky made an awful mistake," Mark Twain told a friend. "He might as well have come over here in his shirttail."

Activities of these kinds were taking their toll on the septuagenarian Mark Twain. When the Robert Fulton Association asked him to address its meeting on April 19 in Carnegie Hall, he accepted, but announced that it would be his last professional public appearance. "Mark Twain's Farewell Lecture" drew a crowded house, made up, said one observer, of "foremost citizens of the republic. They played 'America' as Mark Twain entered and the great audience rose and roared its welcome." Newspapers that day had been filled with horrendous accounts of the San Francisco earthquake the day before, and Mark Twain turned effectively from the kind of humorous rambling with which for forty years he had delighted great audiences by concluding his lecture with a plea for generous aid to the smitten city which as a younger man he had known so well. It seemed appropriate, said commentators, that "Mark Twain's last words on the public platform were an appeal for charity to alleviate human suffering."

"Now," he said to the audience which filled the hall, "since I must, I shall say good-bye. I see many faces in this audience well known to me. They are all my friends, and I feel that those I don't know are my friends too. I wish to consider that you represent the Nation, and that in saying good-bye to you, I am saying good-bye to the Nation."

4

PARTNERS IN CRIME

BUT the nation did not forget Mark Twain. Callers came constantly to 21 Fifth Avenue, and they stayed too long and tired him in spite of the protective guard maintained by his loyal secretary, Isabel Lyon. Since early in the year he had spent at least two hours almost every day dictating a continuation of the autobiography which he had begun during his residence abroad. It was to be a model, he said, for all future autobiographies because of the manner in which "the past and the present are constantly brought face to face" and because "it does not select from my life its showy episodes, but deals merely in the common experiences which go to make up the life of the average human being." He was changing his mind about printing it. "I'd like to see a lot of this stuff in print before I die," he told Henry Rogers, "but not the *bulk* of it, oh no! I'm not desiring to be crucified yet."

He indulged himself now by saying exactly what he thought of people like Bret Harte, Jay Gould, and Andrew Carnegie, about John D. Rockefeller, Jr.'s Baptist Bible class, and about Theodore Roosevelt who seemed to him, *"the* representative American gentleman" because as "a colossal monument visible from all the ends of the earth," he so well represented a nation "by all odds the most ill-mannered . . . that exists on the planet today." And Mark Twain wrote of secret things, like the conspiracy he and Henry Rogers had entered into the summer before, when the financier had made a gift of money to the Reverend Joseph Twichell in Mark Twain's name. "I will supply the money," he had said to Clemens, "and you will do the giving." It amused Mark Twain to have part in this philanthropic hoax on his old Hartford friend, but it worried him also because the Twichells were embarrassingly grateful and wrote him warm letters of thanks. He sent the letters on to Henry Rogers: "I am hurrying them off to you," he wrote, "because I dasn't read them again! I should blush to my heels to fill up with this unearned gratitude again, pouring out of the grateful hearts of those poor swindled people who do not suspect you, but honestly believe I gave the money."

Mary Benjamin Rogers seems to have known this secret also, one of many which she enjoyed sharing with her Uncle Mark. She was, he said, his "dear little partner in crime." And the prank played on their clergyman friend delighted her as much as it did her generous father-in-law. "It would be a crime," Henry Rogers wrote, "to let the Twichells think that you have in any way deceived them." Just look innocent, he advised Mark Twain, "and tell the truth *as you usually do* when you think you can avoid detection."

Conspiracies of this kind were, of course not to be revealed publicly. But friends who had seen other parts of the autobiography, or who had heard of it, encouraged Mark Twain to release at least selected portions. He wrote of it to Henry Rogers: "Howells *thinks* the Auto[biography] will outlive the *Innocents Abroad* a thousand years, and I know it will. I would like the literary world to see (as Howells says) that the *form* of this book is one of the most memorable literary inventions of the ages. And so it is. It ranks with the steam engine, the printing press, and the electric telegraph. I'm the only person who has ever found out the way to build an autobiography."

He worked meanwhile on other writings. *Eve's Diary* was prepared for early summer publication. And Mark Twain was enthusiastic, for a while, about his projected part in a composite novel to be called *The Whole Family*, which Howells, Mary Wilkins Freeman, John Kendrick Bangs, Henry James, Henry Van Dyke, and others would put together, each contributing one chapter.

When he went in May to Dublin again for another long summer among the New Hampshire hills, Mark Twain continued his daily dictation, shuffling in carpet slippers along the veranda of his house as he reminisced or exploded in indignation. One day Albert Bigelow Paine took a series of seven pictures of him as he sat there in his favorite rocking chair, and Mark Twain liked them so well that he had sets of them made up for his friends, each labeled "The Progress of a Moral Purpose." One went to Henry Rogers, another to Mary.

Now and then during the summer Mark Twain made trips to New York, on business with his publishers or to lighten his loneliness with an evening among friends. On the way, he often stopped at Henry Rogers's summer place at Fairhaven, for rest, companionship, but especially, he liked to pretend, for a game of billiards. At Hartford he had had a table of his own, but that had been ten years ago, and he missed it. Mrs. Rogers planned to make him a gift of a new table for Christmas. But it was only summer now, and

Christmas seemed a long way off. Mary Rogers joined her irrepressible Uncle Mark by suggesting that if the gift were to be given at all it might just as well be given quickly.

And there were occasional cruises that summer on the *Kanawha*, sometimes to New York, and once to Bar Harbor, where he and Mary had some kind of a spoofing good time at a luncheon party, conspiring against the others by making a game out of using long words which they pretended no one but themselves could understand. Young in spirit, in spite of his rheumatism and his cough, Mark Twain seems to have enjoyed nothing better than conspiring with young Harry Rogers and his wife against the old folks. They were related, Mary said, because in Eve they had a common ancestor.

Something of the carefree spirit of these visits with the Rogerses is preserved in a note which Mark Twain, having left Fairhaven, wrote to his hostess. In the hurry of packing, "thinking about theology and not noticing," he had inadvertently stuffed into his valise some things which were not his own: "Two books, Mr. Rogers's brown slippers, and a ham." He had thought the ham was his because "it looks like one we used to have." But do not be alarmed, he told Mrs. Rogers, "I will send some of the things back . . . if there is some that won't keep."

But even more revealing of the relationship between Mark Twain and the young people of the Rogers family are the letters which he wrote to Mary during that summer, and in which he reminisced playfully about their adventures. He was discouraged, increasingly unwell, and increasingly lonely. His daughter Clara remained at Norfolk, in quiet retirement, under a physician's care. Jean was with him at Dublin, but she also was never completely well. She was subject to melancholy moods and was much by herself, "dressed always in white, and she was tall and pale and classically beautiful, and she was often silent like a spirit." But Mary Benjamin Rogers, now twenty-five years old and the mother of a small boy and a smaller girl, remained alert and pulsatingly alive. She was playmate, conspirator, and he called her his niece, but she was a surrogate daughter besides. Having returned to Dublin after a visit to Fairhaven, he wrote her on August 4, 1906:

Dublin, New Hampshire
August 4, 1906

You are a very dear partner in crime, and if you have missed me half as much as I have missed you, I am very well satisfied—and pretty vain, too, besides. You've got some exceeding new words, and they are genuine, too—I've verified them by the dictionary, and adopted them. Do you know, by and by none but the most learned people will be able to understand you and me. The others will be awed when they listen: they will think we are talking a foreign language. Awed, and envious and hostile—but no matter, they will admire, anyway. It is good that you are going to practice-up on billiards. We'll have strenuous tournaments at 21; and I hope the table will be exactly the size of the one at Fairhaven, then you won't have to learn the angles all over again. Stick to the English game; you will have a chance to rest while I am making exhibition-runs, and your strength will last the longer, whereas "Chicago" permits no rest.

Colonel Harvey has been here three days, and things have happened! It's a secret—his secret—but no matter, I'll tell it to you: Sept. 1 the North American Review is going to burst upon the world as a fortnightly! and it will contain a purely literary section—that's good, isn't it—and also some

other new features. I think it will be a great magazine, and
I'm charmed. You must be, too—do you hear? He has been
exasperatingly indifferent about my Autobiography, and he
came up here as ca'm as Marjory Fleming's mother-turkey,
to see if he could find a chapter in it good enough for his
literary section. He found twenty-four—to start with. That's
a year's lot. That's the kind of fulsome flattery that I like.
I have written Clara that she can take the money and build
a house with it. The twenty-four chapters make 100,000
words. Then Harvey went on and read the remaining 150,000
words, and has carried the whole of the MS. to Howells,
so that he can do some more selecting. You have already
suspected that my courage about sending it to you had oozed
out—and in truth it had. But I wouldn't be afraid now, if I
had it, for I am sure you wouldn't be a less charitable critic
than Harvey. I'll make bold to put a small strain on you, anyway. I have ordered the September installment to be type-
written in duplicate, so that I can mail it to you. It is only
five ordinary magazine pages—5,000 words. I think you won't
mind that.

I like this arrangement, and so will Mr. Rogers; but he
didn't much like the idea of McClure's newspaper syndicate,
and I ceased to like it myself and stopped the negotiations
before I left New York. I think you will approve it too—at
any rate you must say so. Being my pal, it's your duty.

You'll take the seven pictures? Good. Now don't you re-
pent and back out.

I've a pang! Do you remember about that composite story,
into which I was to add a boy's version? Well, that boy has
not yet knocked at my mind for admission. It means that he
is not interested. Of course, then, he would not tell his story
himself, and I should have to do it for him. I wouldn't ever

do such a thing as that. So I shan't wait on the boy any longer, but will let Miss Lyon write Miss Jourdain to-day and say I can't join Howells and the others in that scheme. I am very glad I made no promises, for now I don't have to break any.

I've got to go to Fairhaven for a day, about the end of this month, unless the heads of the house will come 'mobiling up here, which I hope they will. Will they, do you think? I have to talk with one or another of you about a matter that can't wait very long—in fact it ought to be now, or as close to now as possible. If they can't come, will you and Harry? That would answer perfectly well. For it's another secret— and concerns Mr. Rogers—and I've got to get at it without letting him find out. (Don't you tell him that, and put him on the alert; and don't tell Mrs. Rogers; nor anybody—not even Harry, unless he resorts to violence, the way he did that night when nobody wasn't doing no harm.) Be good, and come along—it will be a delightful journey. I started to write you yesterday but was interrupted.

Oh, if we can only learn to be good, and go to heaven! (There's seven Sabbaths per week, there, I know. To break.) It just makes a body's mouth water. Do you believe the angels are galactophorous? I hope so.

Now, then, on top of all these important things there's still another which . . . . sho! paper of this size doesn't hold anything.

Why, so she was your grandmother! Mine, too. It makes us cousins or something, and I think it's very nice.

Good-bye, dear pal.

S.L.C.

Won't you please mail the enclosed to Mrs. Coe for me?

Sunday

P.S. No, gentle pal, return it to me, in the enclosed envelop. I will go over it again (aloud, this time, which is the only sure test), before I ship it to Harvey.

(Don't let any outsider see it, it is dangersome.)   *S.L.C.*

What he enclosed for Mary Rogers's sister-in-law, Mai Rogers Coe, is not revealed. It may have been a scrap of the autobiography or it may have been some other piece of writing, perhaps even a portion of *What Is Man?*, which at just this time was being printed privately in an edition of two hundred and fifty copies. The proposed publication of the autobiography in the *North American Review* provided Mark Twain with a substantial windfall—$30,000, which he would apply, as he wrote to Mary, to the building of what he told Howells he would call his "Autobiography House" on the wooded acres which at Paine's suggestion he had purchased that spring near Redding, Connecticut. John Mead Howells, his old friend's son, was engaged as architect. Clara went out to see the property and select amid its seventy-five acres the site where the house could most effectively be built. For Mark Twain was convinced now that his problem of where to live was solved. He would retire to a solitude near enough to the exciting maelstrom of New York life to allow him to bask in the strong sunlight of public admiration whenever he wished to take an hour's train ride.

Eve's Diary had been reprinted in June from *Harper's Magazine* into a handsome little book, generously and chastely illustrated by Lester Ralph. Mary Rogers read her copy with interest, especially Adam's description of his mate: "She is all interest, eagerness, vivacity, the world is to her

a charm, a wonder, a mystery, a joy . . . she is color mad
. . . she is a quite remarkably comely creature—lithe,
slender, rounded, shapely, nimble, graceful . . . beautiful."
She playfully accused her Uncle Mark of having described
her as the young Eve. On August 14, he replied:

> Dublin, New Hampshire
> August 14, 1906

Ho, you miraculous combination of quicksilver, watch-
springs and sunshine, how you do dance out from your pen
and light up this solemn solitude and set things amoving!
No matter how long you live you'll never get old, (thanks
be!). My wife never did, neither did my mother; and my
mother lived to be 88, and always she was all animation and
champagne and charm, like you. I think it a most remarkable
thing that I was able to draw you (as mother Eve) to the
very life, and all by accident. From the first page to the last,
there you are; it is your very self, exactly as you would have
looked and acted if you had been Eve, with a spang-new beautiful world to flutter around in—and not a detail of you
lacking, so far as I can see, but the tawny hair and the clothes.
And on pages 69 and 71 you are concentrated. I am pretty
proud of that accident. No doubt, accidents that approximate
it have happened in literature, but this isn't an approximation, it is a reproduction, and stands all by itself, unfellowed.

Miss Lyon went to New York yesterday, to be gone a week
and more, and meet Clara there and help her and the archi-
tect plan the new house, and see that there is a proper
billiard-room in it for you to break records in; Jean has gone
with twelve young people to climb Monadnock; so the place
is empty and still, and that is the solemn solitude I have

The life and spirit that endeared Mary to her Uncle Mark are
caught in this photograph.

Mary Benjamin Rogers and Harry Rogers on their honeymoon.

spoken of. Would you believe it?—I am developing into a tramper of the woods myself. The rich twilight of these lonely woodland roads is enchanting. If you would come—but I perceive that you can't. Day before yesterday I covered a very handsome distance indeed, for a novice.

I am so glad you liked that scrap of autobiography, dear pal; and I wish I could send more, since you are willing to read it, but there's only one "set" here, for Harvey carried away the other set to select installments from. Some day it will come back, and then I will overwhelm you with it unless you stop trying to make out that you are a fictitious pal. There isn't any way for you to be fictitious. You wouldn't know how to go about it. Do you know?—I had the delightfulest letter from your Merlie, and I was smart enough to read between the lines that she was really grateful to us for keeping order in that bridge party; and she as good as said she wished she could have all her bridge orgies policed and tranquillized like that. These are not her exact words, but they are very close.

As to that secret. I must manage that—and soon. But how? I have to have your criminal help. I could go to Fairhaven day after tomorrow (Thursday)—and Friday just as well—but shall you be there? And will uncle Henry come up Friday? (He mustn't be allowed to escape to the mountains before this conspiracy is consummated—indeed that won't do!—do you hear, Spontaneous Combustion, do you?)

Will you telegraph or telephone me?

But if you find it must be put off a week, I will arrange accordingly. Meantime keep your eye on the head senior, and see that he doesn't flee to the mountains.

From all accounts of the cruise, you and Harry must have

had a delightful time; and not such a very unsociable time, neither.

If I may have the privilege, dear pal, I also am
Yours affectionately

S.L.C.

All this time, I've had the help of three kittens—and not dead ones, either

Merlie was the affectionate name which her step-children and step-in-laws and step-grandchildren all called Henry Rogers's second wife, Emile Augusta Randel Rogers. The nature of the order which Mark Twain and Mary kept at her bridge party can be imagined but not certainly established. The kittens, however, can be identified. They were named, the three of them, Sackcloth and Ashes—one was Sackcloth and the other two, which looked exactly alike, were both named Ashes. Mark Twain had rented them at Dublin for the summer because he thought it cruel to own cats which he could not keep or would not be allowed to take back to New York with him for the winter. They provided constant amusement, frolicking about his feet as he walked the veranda dictating, climbing into his lap as he sat watching the evening lights over Monadnock, and one even intruded to the series of photographs which Paine had taken of him in his rocking chair.

Proofs for the autobiography as it was to appear in print now began to come in. It must have been on another visit to Fairhaven that Mark Twain and Mary looked them over together, pausing with special interest over the editorial comment which Colonel Harvey had prepared for the issue in which the first installment would appear. They pretended to be dissatisfied with the generously flattering remarks there

made about Mark Twain's "humor preeminent, wit un-
excelled, philosophy rare," about "his mind . . . so clear, his
heart so strong, and his art so masterful." The autobiography was praised as "wonderful because of its truth, its
frankness, its unhesitating and unrestricted human feeling."
On returning to Dublin, Mark Twain wrote her about it on
August 25 in a letter which he apparently kept by his bedside,
adding to it a page or a paragraph, perhaps even only a sentence at a time between bouts of dictating. Instead of mailing it to Fairhaven, he sent it addressed to "Mr. or Mrs.
H. H. Rogers, Jr., Yacht *Kanawha*, Yacht Club Pier, Foot of
23d St.," with a note on the envelop requesting, "Please send
this aboard the yacht and greatly oblige, Mark Twain." The
letter, thus specially delivered, reads:

> *Dublin, New Hampshire*
> *August 25, 1906*
> *Saturday*

*Now this can't wait, but must be attended to at once, O
dear pal and incomparable niece! I am still troubled about
those editorial remarks about me which we read in proof
yesterday. Naturally it would not be quite delicate in me to
move in the matter, yet I feel that something ought to be
done. Now my idea is that you could do it, with perfect
propriety. Suppose you write Col. Harvey something like this:*

*Dear Sir: If my uncle knew that I was writing you upon
this matter he would disapprove, for he is very delicate in
his feelings; so I will ask you not to let him learn about it.
To me your praises of him seemed most generous—indeed
prodigal, even extravagant; but he is so sensitively organized
that to him they sounded cold and indifferent, and they
deeply saddened him. He is almost morbidly fond of com-*

pliments, and he realizes that these are good ones, but thinks
they are over-cautious and thin. When we of the family
butter him we do not do it with a knife, we use a trowel. It
will profoundly gratify him if you will allow me to add the
following paragraph to what you have written.

Very truly yours,

Mary Rogers

That is the idea, dear. Just write him that, then follow
it with the paragraph. A warm one, you understand. And
send me a copy of it, so that I can catch him if he tries to
leave out any of the adjectives. Do it yourself, dear; don't let
Harry help, nor uncle Henry, for they are prejudiced. There
will be plenty of time, for the issue-date has been postponed
to Sept. 7. I know, for I have just read the proof of the "Virginia-Clemens" installment. A duplicate has gone to Fairhaven, but I don't need it and you can burn it.

It is past noon, now, and time to get up and dress for
MacVeagh's luncheon-party. I am going to walk, one way,
through the woods—it's only a mile. Then there's a lecture
at the Club at 4. I'm going to interrupt it.

I'm dressed, now. When I looked in the glass I was stunned
with admiration; and it seemed to me that if I could have a
grandfather like that I could die happy.

It was a gay luncheon and a good lecture. I shall lecture,
myself, at the Club soon. I mean to call for a text, and teach
the art of after-dinner speaking. Come—so that I can illus-
trate the blush-science.

Shucks, Clara isn't going to sing in Norfolk—so that's off.

Sunday, noon

It is nearly time to get (temporarily) up. Jean came in at
8:30 and delivered her budget of news; Miss Lyon followed
with the letters, and the rest of the news. This is a very
remarkable society here and you would like it and feel at
home in it. Professor Pumpelly and wife, learned people; Mr.
Secretary Hitchcock, the best man in the Roosevelt cabinet,
I think; several Yale and Harvard professors; two historians—
Hart and Henderson; Wm. Cabot, explorer of the Great
Lone Land; Handyside Cabot and wife—music and art; Joe
Smith, artist and playwright; George Brush, artist of high
repute and an able and interesting talker; Abbott Thayer,
capable artist, and discoverer of Nature's real color-scheme
for the protection of the animals; his daughter, aged twenty,
a very gifted artist; Colton Greene, author—and so on. I wish
you would come and get acquainted. Say the word, Mary! At
MacVeagh's luncheon yesterday there was only one idiot.
This average cannot be matched anywhere, perhaps.*

Miss Lyon told of a very remarkable exhibition of spirit
and character (a duplicate of an exhibition of your own),
on the part of a girl-friend of yours. And of course her name
is Stewart! It does seem to me that the Stewarts have all
gotten loose this year. Isn't it curious? Finally—a minute ago
—Miss Lyon opened up on Nietsche; I can't stand Nietsche,
so I dismissed her with some Don't-Mary words suitable to
the provocation, and I think there won't be any more
Nietsche to-day.

I think I will talk at the Country Club next Saturday, and
in the village the following Saturday (Sept. 8). There's a
concert (the one I spoke of) on Friday the 7th in the great
room at MacVeagh's house, and it will be fine. Do come;

I can easily put off both talks until October. Come along,
Spontaneous Combustion; be good and don't say no.

Did I give you the valuable nonsense-verses I wrote about
you in Fairhaven?

* My child, you mustn't say "Were you the one?" For that is the
obvious remark. It is so obvious that it would occur to the cat. Don't
ever make the obvious remark, if you can stop yourself in time. Leave
it to the dull-witted—or to the untrained, shall I say? You are not dull-
witted, you are bright; and in the mouths of such the obvious remark
is always a crime. And in speaking, do not permit yourself to deal in
commonplace phrasing. However, you are not guilty of that, you use
higher forms; and so this is not an accusation, it is only a reminder.
That idiot desolated me with commonplace forms, and with the obvious
remark, all through that bright (and often brilliant) luncheon-talk. She
was just deadly. It was like sitting beside a persistent and unpleasant
odor. Am I too officious, dear, in intruding my wisdom and schoolings
upon you? Don't be offended, I am not meaning any harm or any dis-
courtesy. Uncles, through pride in their high place, are rather too apt
to play preceptor, I am aware of that. I am thankful that you have dis-
carded slang. You have goodness in abundance; you have native frankness and sincerity; you have high ideals—qualities, these, of the clean
mind and the clean heart: slang has no place in that regal company.

Monday noon

I have just finished dictating the conspiracy-installment,
and have put in the Prince of Wales and General Grant—
and also a word about W. W. Jacobs's delightful "Dialstone
Lane." It will go to you soon, and you will sound the Admiral when he comes. There's no hurry; take your time about
it. That is, about that; but I hope you won't take too much
time about sending me a letter. In the Grant anecdote another Stewart turns up—Stewart of Nebraska.

3 p.m.—in bed

I have resumed my habits, you see. When I am not
away from home I live in bed, to beat the lonesomeness. Now

then, Mariechen, I have just finished re-reading this Con-spiracy-MS which you and I read together, and I believe that the addition of today's dictation will round it symmetrically out and make it readable and discursive, and cover up all signs of intention. Polish up your diplomacies, sweet pal, sweetest of pals, and prepare to beat down and defeat all the Admiral's objections!

Tuesday, 12:50 noon

I have been dictating for an hour and thirty-five minutes. And what is that to you? Ordinarily it wouldn't be anything to you, of course, but maybe it's different this time, because part of it is about our Bar Harbor luncheon. Maybe you will strike it out, but no names are mentioned, and I don't be-lieve you will; I think you will let it stay.

I miss you—dear me, yes!

Affectionately, your uncle

Mark

It must have been Marian Stewart of New York, with whom Mary Rogers had gone to school, who put on the remarkable exhibition of spirit and character of which Miss Lyon spoke, but on what occasion or for what purpose is not known. The Stewart mentioned later in the letter in con-nection with the Grant anecdote was undoubtedly Senator William Stewart with whom Clemens had served briefly and unhappily as a secretary almost forty years before. Mark Twain was evidently at work on sections of the autobiog-raphy of which he suspected the Admiral—that is, Henry Rogers, who was also the Uncle Henry mentioned earlier in the letter—would not approve. The *"Don't*-Mary" words

with which Mark Twain dismissed his secretary when she
began to talk of Nietzsche—whose name he could not spell
any better than most of us can—were without doubt in-
spirationally profane. There seems to have been a private
joke between Mary and her Uncle Mark that there were
certain words of his which when uttered drew from her an
admonishing "Don't!" But the phrase seems sometimes to
have meant, not only " 'Don't say that,' said Mary," but
also " 'Don't say that, Mary,' said your Uncle Mark." It was
a favorite secret joke between them.

Mark Twain, as has been seen, was proud of his Dublin
neighbors. Secretary of the Interior Ethan Allen Hitchcock,
Raphael Pumpelly, the geologist, just returned from explora-
tion in Central Asia for the Carnegie Museum, and Franklin MacVeagh, who would become Secretary of the Treasury
in Taft's cabinet, were men of about his age, active, successful, and excellent companions. Others, like Albert Bushnell
Hart of Harvard and Ernest Flagg Henderson, another his-
torian, were younger by almost twenty years, as were the
artists and musicians who helped liven the summer colony
there. They had pleasant times together, with local lectures
such as that one which Mark Twain threatened to interrupt,
and private charades. Mark Twain's old friend Melville
Stone, head of the Associated Press, was soon to arrive.
Young people, like his own daughter Jean and Abbott
Thayer's talented daughter provided additional outlets for
Mark Twain's public ebullience. When he wrote Mary Rogers
again on August 28, he spoke about the article which Colonel
Harvey had written to praise him and he told also of some
of the good times to be had in Dublin:

Dublin, New Hampshire
August 28, 1906

Oh, don't mind me, dear! I love to see you flash and sparkle and frisk about and carry on, even when the inspiration of it is malice and I'm the butt!

PARABLE

All on a summer's day an obese and bristly great tarantula was resting and reflecting upon his merits, with his body crouched against the ground and his several elbows sticking up, whereby one perceived that his aspect was historical and duplicated the wreck of the Maine. Anon came a golden-belted little wasp frisking by, sweet and dear and winsome and aware of it; and he, being without discretion, begged her to furnish him some compliments wherewith to warm up a cold eulogium. But she, mistaking his desire, and supposing he wanted facts, complied, with glad enthusiasm, and walked all over him from stem to rudder-post and from futtock-shroud to garboard strake, and wheresoever she found a defect in him she darted her stiletto into it and made him shrivel!

MORAL

What have facts to do with a eulogium?

Now aren't you conscienceless, to expose me so to the Colonel! The first you know, history will repeat itself and you will get your deserts:

> But too late they saw their error,
> And to little Mary's terror,
> She was shoved with ignominy from the room.

Don't you fret about your diplomacy; what you couldn't accomplish there, nobody could. Therefore you did the best that could be done, and you have my cordial and prodigal thanks. You are a loyal and faithful conspirator, and it is a pleasure to conspire with you.

TELEGRAMS

Your niece's eulogium will destroy you. Get her to withdraw it. Harvey.

What is the matter with it? Mark.

How can you ask? Harvey.

I have read it several times, and liked it better each time. Mark.

But it will destroy the mag. Harvey.

Oh, d—— the mag. Mark.

Do at least get her to modify it. Harvey.

Do you know her? Mark.

No, Why? Harvey.

It would delight her to death. Yes, she would "modify" it. She would put in the rest of the facts. Don't hunt up opportunities for her, Harvey, she doesn't need any of your help. Mark.

Tomorrow the premier of England will be 70. A London paper has asked for "cables" from friends. I've sent one:

"To the Prime Minister: Congratulations, not condolences. Before seventy we are merely respected, and we have to behave, to keep that asset; but after seventy we are respected, esteemed, admired, revered, and do not have to behave unless we want to. When I first knew you, one of us was not even respected. Mark Twain."

Come, do a pal's duty—say it's sweet; I'm perishing for butter.

Oh, as to "second-bests," I have them, but what of that? You ought to reflect that there's a pretty wide interval between first-bests and second-bests.

The conspiracy installment will go into the Autobiography just as it stands. But it won't appear until I am dead, then he won't mind. I don't believe I sent you the "Virginia-Clemens" chapter, Mary dear; I think Harvey was pressed for time.

I ought not to admire and applaud your scandalous eulogy, but it is captivatingly breezy and flowing and happily phrased and veracious and malicious and good.

Times are brisking up. Last Saturday I appeared on the platform with two pupils, and asked for a text. This one was furnished: "If it were decreed that one of the sexes must be extinquished, which one would it be best to spare?" We debated it for an hour and a quarter on the lines of my Spontaneous-Oratory-System-Without-Preparation, and it was a gay and noisy time. Tuesday night there was a very bright play by a lad of eighteen, and it was done in exceedingly good style by a dozen lads and lassies, none [of] them older than the author. We had a luncheon-gang to-day. There's a local-talent concert tomorrow, and charades at Professor Pumpelly's Saturday night, and I'm to be in it in my two admired characters (the German Emperor—drunk—and a baby nine months old). Notwithstanding these enlivenments, I miss my pal. I returned, a little while ago (5:30) from my daily compulsory long tramp through the woods.

6 p.m.

Some visitors are announced; I must get up and dress and go down.

6:25

That's done. I dictated two hours this morning. I am an industrious person, and entitled to great praise. Furnish it! Butter!

It is lovely of you to write me such nice long letters, and I *thank you ever so much. Twice you have apologized for this grace. You mustn't.*

I have promised by telegraph to speak at the dinner of the "Associated Liars" as you irreverently call them, Sept. 19. My idea is to go to Boston Saturday, the 15th, rest there, and go on to New York the next day. Clara will be there and will go to Norfolk the 19th—where she is to sing on the 22d. I'll slip up there unbeknownst, if you'll go with me? Won't Harry go, too? It's bound to be interesting. Clara dreads to have me present, but she hasn't asked me not to come, in so many words.

Later. A telegram from Clara; she has gone home—too cold in Norfolk.

No Melville Stone, so far, he is lost or mislaid, I reckon.

It is holiday, to-day, but we need another charade for to-night, and women must work and men must pray, you know. How useful the dictionary is! I opened it and found a charade-combination right away, to wit, life-like. I know it will play!

First Division—"Life" (human)

An oriental well; procession of Arabic pilgrims arriving, silent, worn, weary, sad; a halt; they drink, pass on, and disappear—a voice chanting—(the chanter not visible)—A moment's Halt, a momentary Taste (and the rest of the quatrain).

Second Division—"Like"

Unhappy courting scene. Text for elaboration: "We must part; it is irrevocable; I did like you; and but for that episode I could have loved you, in time, but now I do not even like you."

Dramatis Personae: Clemens and Gladys Thayer.

The Whole—"Life-like"

Curtain raises on a marble bust—(Jean, white-enameled). Draped in coarse studio-sheer from breast to feet. Nobody present; no words; silence for two minutes—then curtain descends.

If I only had my pal to plead with, in the middle scene! Gladys will do gravity, earnestness, the hurt heart and all that, ever so well, but she lacks variety. Bless your soul, you don't!

Jean's finely chiseled statuesque face will be just stunning, in cold marble.

That afternoon concert was fine.

This is no holiday!—I will rise and dress. Turn and turn about it has been Jean, then Miss Lyon, then Jean again, all the morning—getting instructions about the charades. Charades are exceedingly important events, Mamma Eve.

I am very glad you take my criticisms in such good part. I shan't ever hurt you with them wittingly, dear niece of mine.

Your affectionate uncle,

Mark

Only one of Mary Rogers's "nice long letters" survives, but it provides convincing evidence of the talented verve which attracted Mark Twain to her. From Fairhaven she wrote:

Fairhaven, Massachusetts
September 9, 1906

Today being Sunday dear Uncle Methuselah my thoughts, by antithesis, naturally revert to you, and you season the day for me, not disagreeably you understand, but just tempering my mind to a comfortable wickedness—

You know I do like to write to you so much!—for several reasons, the first because it is not a duty and the big principal reason is that now I have the field undisturbed and unrestricted and no matter what I say you can't stop me, or answer back—until the return mail—and by that time my ire will be past and I will be "busy" over some other reform. As a rule I don't care for one-sided conversations—(Harry would "butt in" here if he had a chance)—you see there's the joy—no interruption, no interference. It's a fine feeling, and if I only could think of something scandalous and dreadful to say—to make you gasp! it would be just perfect—but I can't.

Monday morning, and a nice long fat letter from my pal— I do love the "return mail."

Your abnormal hunger for Butter is perfectly shocking! "I'm perishing for Butter—" you write (now don't interrupt me)—the truth was I did not think you could possibly digest any more after that fatty-degenerating article of Colonel Harvey's—so I gave you course number five. with French dressing instead. Of course I know that "Bacon and Butter are two of the most easily assimilated fats" for so says our learned physician Quintard. Still even nourishing foods can be overdone and a line must be drawn somewhere. I do not think you are old enough yet to always know what is best for you. Most people are attracted by your winning ways and are very prone to over indulge you, but I, as your pal, have your nobler interests at heart and want to mold and strengthen your moral character, so am going to put you on a diet of

Truthful Steaks and Facts boiled **down**. They supply stamina to the most jaded constitutions.

I heard Millicent say to Billy Coe yesterday "Muddie said No, Billy, she would not give me another chocolate, and I will not ask her again, it would be very rude." So I do not think it would be delicate for you to mention "Butter" again, do you?

Remember this disciplining is "for your own good" and "It hurts me more than it does you."

Father R. said he had a telegram from you last night saying you were going to New York this week—I suppose you will not return to Dublin again this year, will you? We expect to move into our Tuxedo house about October first. I doubt if it will be sufficiently settled for the children before that. Most of our furniture goes out next week.

Are you really going to Norfolk? We promised a man in Tuxedo last Spring to go to Garden City for the Automobile races and I believe the first ones are on the 22nd of September. About ten young people are going in his party. He has hired a house for us. Everyone is very keen about it. I think the races will be very stupid, but I don't say so above a whisper—and eliminating the main attraction the party ought to be great fun.

So you are to speak at Melville Stone's dinner. Good! I wish I were to be there. I have been reading the "Virginia-Clemens installment"—and enjoyed it very much. I see they have you down in large type as the chief attraction—(isn't it balm to your soul?)—

I have also been reading "G's" article on "Mr. Roosevelt's Right to Accept a Renomination" and think he goes far towards proving his hero an untrustworthy knave, inadvertently, of course—or rather I mean, unintentionally.

Goodbye—Yours Affectionately,

Mary Rog.

P.S. added to Telegram sent to the Premier of England on the occasion of his celebrating his seventieth birthday.

Dear Primey—

Just a line more to say that I cherish no hard feeling towards you, nor have I ever envied you your hih lif position in society—to be obliged to lug around the title of Minister, even though it is of the premier class would have taken the heart clean out of me and life would have lost its savour. You've earned a just reward and a crown in a happier land.

May you find them soon.

Mark Twain

I do like your telegram best.

"Our learned physician Quintard," of whom Mary Rogers spoke, was Dr. Edward Quintard of New York, physician to the Rogers family, who was later to become Mark Twain's physician also. Millicent, who gave a lesson in etiquette to Billy Coe, was Mary Rogers's young daughter, and Billy was her five-year-old nephew, William Rogers Coe. The article about Theodore Roosevelt's right to seek renomination had appeared in the September 15 issue of the *North American Review*.

As Mark Twain continued his autobiography, leisurely dictating about 1,500 words each day, he kept adding to it by inserting what he called "fat" to the manuscript, slipping in "old pigeon-holed things, of the years gone by, which I or the editors didn't dasn't print." Among them was the little book about *Captain Stormfield's Visit to Heaven*, "which I read you," he told Howells, "in Hartford about thirty years ago and which you said 'publish.' It reads quite well to me," he continued, "without altering a word, now that it isn't to see print until I am dead."

But as he read it again now in the late summer of 1906, it seemed too good to keep in manuscript. He apparently sent it off then to George Harvey of Harper's, asking his opinion. In an undated letter, probably written early in September, Colonel Harvey replied:

Dear Uncle Mark

I have just visited Heaven with the cap'n—His account seems exact, truthful and, as you say, godly—too damn godly [here Mark Twain has scrawled "(Don't, Mary!)" above the last two words] *for a secular paper like the Magazine—I'm sure it wouldn't do to print it now and I guess you're sure too, if you'll tell the truth* [here Mark Twain has written "(Naughty Mabel!)"].

The first review is out today and in a few days I'll send you what they all say about it.

I think it's pretty good.

When are you coming home?

G. H.

By the "first review" it is assumed that Colonel Harvey meant the September 7 issue of the *North American Review* which would contain the first installment of Mark Twain's autobiography. Mark Twain made notes on the letter as he passed it along to his secretary: "Tell him I arrive Monday 17th. Give him some abuse about the Horse's Tale illustrations"—"The Horse's Tale" had appeared in two parts in

Harper's Magazine in August and September, and something about Lucius Wolcott Hitchcock's illustrations apparently did not please Mark Twain. Write the letter, he told his secretary, "in the first person and I will sign it—not today, but in the morning. *Tell him I arrive 6 p.m.* (It's a hint; I reckon he'll know enough to recognize *that*.)"

Then he sent the letter on to Mary Rogers—writing in his "*Don't*, Mary" and "*Naughty* Mabel," and explaining to her:

You see, dear, your eulogium has scared him: he's afraid of everything now, even theological disquisitions. This one was written thirty-eight years ago and is still over-warm apparently. He wanted to see it (for the Xmas Harper). Well, he has seen it.

U. M.

Colonel Harvey was to change his mind, for the story of Captain Stormfield's visit would appear in *Harper's Magazine* a year later, in the December, 1907, and January, 1908, issues. But now Mark Twain was busy with other things. As his recent letters to Mary Rogers had suggested, there had been some question of whether Clara Clemens would be well enough to give a concert in Norfolk, but finally it was settled, that she would, at the Gymnasium there, on Saturday evening, September 22, 1906, assisted by her friend and fellow student Marie Nichols, a violinist, and accompanied by her teacher Isidore Luckstone.

In a letter begun at Dublin on September 21 and continued at intervals during the next two days, Mark Twain tells of preparations for the occasion and of the concert itself. He wrote on whatever scraps of paper came readily to hand. The first part of the letter is written across the face of a typed note from W. M. Van der Weyde, whose letterhead describes him as "Photographer of Celebrities" doing business at 145 Fifth Avenue. His letter, dated September 21, reads:

VAN DER WEYDE

PHOTOGRAPHER OF CELEBRITIES

145 FIFTH EVENUE

NEW YORK

September 21, 1906

Dear Mr. Clemens:

The editor of The Reader magazine has asked me to make a new photograph of you, provided of course you will consent.

I bring this note to your house myself, bringing at the same time my camera, in the hope that you can spare a few moments this afternoon.

I will not use flashlight at all, employing only the ordinary daylight, and I shall take only about five minutes of your time.

Faithfully yours,

W. M. Van der Weyde

Permission was given, and the ordeal proved not to be unpleasant, nor the results without merit.

21 Fifth Avenue

September 21, 1906

At 3 p.m., I put Clara in her coupé and started her for Norfolk, then I undressed and went to bed, bringing with me, from my handbag, Clara's most recent letter, Jean's most recent, and yours. I was reading yours when the photographer entered the room. I dropped my hand and looked up, and he said: "There—don't move—stay just as you are, the letter in your hand—a good pose! looks just as if you'd been interrupted, and wanted to use language!" I said, "Oh, no, nothing severer than 'Don't-Mary'"—and he laughed the laugh which a person laughs when he pretends to understand but knows very well he doesn't. He made half a dozen negatives and said he would have a couple of finished pictures waiting me at the house on my return from Norfolk. I want to trade you one for butter.

8 p.m. In Disgrace

I was up and out again at 5 p.m. and called on a lady, and would have stayed to dinner, but didn't, because a pair of distinguished strangers were coming, and this is no weather for exertion, mental or physical. It was providential—for my cravat wasn't tied. I found it out when I got home. I feel very much disgraced. Still, it was not my fault: my pal was far away. Katy was gone to the station with Clara, there was no one to do the tying, no one to stop me on my way out and remind me that I was irregular. Shall I cry? . . . I will think about it.

8:15. In bed, of course

Katy—bearing news—has come up to pack my luggage for the early train. When I was taking leave of Clara I asked her to let me lead her out before her audience. She said, no —"You'll get all the welcome, and I none." But on the way to the station she told Katy she had changed her mind and she would like to be led out by her father! Mariechen, it's butter from the butterless! and very gratifying. Next, there'll be butter from Jean—yes, and even from you; I am not despairing.

Norfolk, 3 p.m., 22d.

I have gone to bed—as usual. It is to be hoped that you are in bed, too, and that last night's hilarious late hours and this morning's murderously early ones have not broken you down utterly and condemned you to Norfolk again.

I had a marvelously narrow escape from death coming up in the train.

Terese has been here interrupting. She is the lovable Tuscan girl we had with us in Florence. She was at the door when I drove up in the downpour, and the tears were running down her face. I said reproachfully, "Terese, I am hurt and I am going away; I never expected to see you cry to see me come." She looked distressed and siezed me by both hands and exclaimed, "Oh, it is not that—it is that I cry for joy to see the signor padrone again!"

That is very nice butter, and I know how to make Terese furnish it; for she believes everything I say. She is smitten with death and doesn't know it; no one would imagine it, for she does not look ill. It is very pathetic.

She came up to unpack my things, and put everything to rights and make me comfortable, and now I shall have to do her work all over again, I think, for she has been so busy talking her captivating broken English for half hour that with all her good intentions she has only arranged to make me uncomfortable—just as happened with my amended button-hole flower Wednesday evening—it was much more to my liking before.

Miss Gordon (of the 69th Street infirmary) was in the

*train, and she had a box of flowers for Clara. Why wasn't
I as thoughtful! It is a shame to be so thoughtless as I am.*

*Clara and I have had a chat. She is in bed; she had a fright
in the train yesterday. She says I mustn't lead her on the
stage; also she says I must. She has a dread that the house will
call for a speech. I said, "I will excuse myself." "But they
won't take the excuse." "Then I will say, 'I would gladly
respond, but Mr. Luckstone, who was to accompany me on
the trombone has unfortunately caught a cold.'" She said
that if I would be sure and stop there—and so forth and so
forth. We had a most entertaining dispute but didn't really
settle anything. I wish you were here, to settle it in your
arbitrary way. We reach New York Sunday eve.*

Mark Twain was careful to let Mary Rogers know that
it was her letter which might appear thus publicly in his
hand. But when his picture appeared in the *Reader* in December, 1906, as Mark Twain's "latest and most striking
portrait," the hand holding the letter did not show, for Mr.
Van der Weyde had developed the photograph so that it
presented only his subject's shaggy head.

The Katy whom Mark Twain mentions as accompanying
Clara to the train and then returning to pack his luggage,
was Katy Leary, a mainstay in the Clemens household for
almost thirty years, as nurse and companion to the girls and
now as their father's housekeeper. She had been with Susy
at her death, and had cared for Mrs. Clemens at Riverdale
and in Florence. Much of the burden of maintaining physical
comforts for Mark Twain fell to her loyal and capable hands.

The next portion of Mark Twain's letter is written across
a sheet of paper which contains pencil scrawls made by
Clara's German maid as she attempted to write down the

contents of congratulatory telegrams as they were transmitted to her over the telephone: "Masch Love and Tauht from Us all Marion Stuart," "N. York. Delaudace Delaudace Ed Ougours Delaudace Jin Howell," "Duylin N H Mey Luve und warmes Wisches fr the best Held vois und gratest Secsess Liv Jean L Cles," and "Wiscasset Main Shool bi with ju in Spirit all Day un Evening braudly and Applauding." Mark Twain translated as "Much love and thought from us all. Marian Stewart," "De l'audace, de l'audace et toujours de l'audace. John Howells," "Dublin, N. H. My love and warmest wishes for the best [health (?)—this word Mark Twain could not decipher], voice, and greatest success. [Love (?)—this he also could not decipher], Jean L. Clemens," and "Wiscasset, Maine. Shall be with you in spirit all day and evening proudly and applauding." He continued his letter to Mary on whatever spaces were left surrounding the messages.

Saturday, 6 p.m.

These are a delight! as you perceive, they are telegrams of hope and encouragement; and as you may guess, they have been taken down, at the telephone, by a German. It is Clara's charming old Frau Bratengeier. The person at the other end of the wire was not a shining helper in the matter. We have had a difficult time over them; and after all, there's still a doubtful word or two for you to shed some light upon.

Midnight. It's over!

Sack, it was a distinct triumph!—an unqualified triumph— a triumph without any alloying doubts hanging about it—a beautiful, and blood-stirring, and spirit-satisfying triumph; and I would rather have lost one of my ears than missed it, and

I would have contributed the other one to have you there.

Everything was in Clara's favor, even to the weather, which was horrible; I was charmed with it and grateful for it, for the delightfulest of all audiences and most inspiring is a bad-weather audience. It doesn't come for fashion's sake or duty's sake, it comes because it wants to! The contrast between that alert and glowing and expectant company and Melville Stone's museum of desiccated mummies was the contrast between the living and the dead. It was all on hand, galleries and all, an hour before the advertised hour (8:30) for the beginning. Rodman Gilder and I arrived at 8:30, according to command, but I was forbidden to enter the green room, and also forbidden to lead Clara out. The manager said no, this was Clara's show and I couldn't steal any part of it. I was given a seat in the third row and admonished to keep quiet and not try to

The next portion of the letter is written on the program of the concert, with instruction to Mary Rogers that it "follows the telegrams," that is, the preceding portion which had been written on Frau Bratengeier's scratch-pad:

attract attention. Luckstone's train was late. He arrived at 9, and presently led Clara out. She was Egyptian and lovely! Sack, you could not have looked lovelier yourself. I knew she was frozen with stage-fright, but she didn't show it.

Before she reached the middle of number one I saw she was going to win. Then Luckstone turned his head and beamed over his shoulder at her, and Miss Gordon, who sat trembling at my side, heaved a deep relief-sigh and whispered, "There—that's approval—she's perfectly safe now."

And so she was. From that time forth to the end she walked in victory. At the end Miss Gordon and I only waited till the house had called her out a couple of times, then we

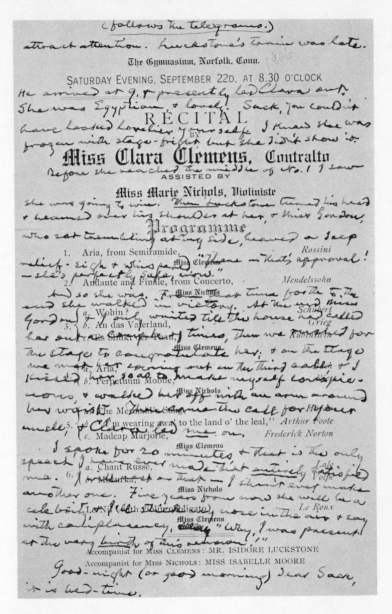

(follows the telegrams.)

attract attention. Luckstone's train was late.

The Gymnasium, Norfolk, Conn.

SATURDAY EVENING, SEPTEMBER 22D, AT 8.30 O'CLOCK

He arrived at 9, & presently led Clara out.
She was Egyptian, & lovely! Sack, you couldn't
have looked lovelier yourself. I knew she was
frozen with stage-fright but she didn't show it.

RECITAL
BY

Miss Clara Clemens, Contralto
ASSISTED BY

Before she reached the middle of No. 1 I saw

Miss Marie Nichols, Violiniste

she was going to win. Then Luckstone turned his head
& leaned over his shoulder at her, & Miss Gordon,
who sat trembling at his side, heaved a deep

Programme

relief. Sick & wins —
— she's perfectly safe now.

1. Aria, from Semiramide,   Rossini
   Miss Clemens   "There — that's approval!"

2. Andante and Finale, from Concerto,   Mendelssohn
   And so she was. From that time forth to the
   Miss Nichols
   end she walked in victory. At the end Miss
   Gordon & I only waited till the house had called
   a. Wohin?   Schubert
3. b. An das Vaterland,   Grieg
   her out a dozen or many times, then we rushed for
   the stage to congratulate her; & on the stage
   Miss Clemens
   we met. Aria, coming out on the third call & I
   b. Perpetuum Mobile,   Miss Nichols
   kissed her, so as to make myself conspicuous, & walked her off with an arm around
   her waist. The Mermaid's Song the call for —
5. b. "I'm wearing away to the land o' the leal," Arthur Foote
   c. Madcap Marjorie,   Frederick Norton
   & Clara led me on.

   I spoke for 20 minutes & that is the only
   a. Chant Russe,   Miss Clemens   Lalo
   speech I have ever made that entirely satisfied
   me. 6. b. Mazurka, so on that — I shan't ever make
   Miss Nichols
   another one. Five years from now she will be a
   celebrity LONG (with Piano obligato), nose in the air & say   Le Roux
   with complacency, "Why, I was present
   at the very birth of this reknown!"

Accompanist for MISS CLEMENS: MR. ISIDORE LUCKSTONE
Accompanist for MISS NICHOLS: MISS ISABELLE MOORE

Good-night (or good morning) dear Sack,
it is bed-time.

Program of Clara Clemens's recital. Mark Twain shared this
happy event with Mary by writing his letter to her on congratulatory telegrams and on the program itself.

BUTTER WANTED

=

Any Kind:

New; Old;

Salted; Unsalted;

Odorless; Fragrant;

Real preferred, but

Oleomargarine not

turned away.

=

Apply at the old stand,

21 Fifth ave.,

at the

Sign of the Butterfly.

Mark Twain's requirement of "butter" was a favorite joke between him and Mary.

rushed to the stage to congratulate her; and on the stage we met her coming out on the third call; I kissed her so as to make myself courageous, and walked her off with an arm around her waist. Then came the call for your uncle, and Clara led me on.

I spoke for twenty minutes, and that is the only speech I have ever made that entirely satisfied me. I shall rest on that —I shan't ever make another one. Five years from now she will be a celebrity, and I'll stick my nose in the air and with complacency, "Why, I was present at the very birth of this renown!"

Good-night (or good morning) dear Sack; it is bed-time.

Sunday, 10 a.m.

I perceive that you are not writing me yet, about your auto-adventures. But you are better employed I think—and hope—sleeping and resting.

Twelve or fifteen New York friends came up, and about the same number from Hartford. Clara will repeat in Hartford pretty soon, and in Providence two or three weeks hence.

She satisfied Mr. Bacon her manager, last night. Perhaps that was the main triumph. I hear Clara's voice downstairs—there is nothing melancholy about it. It is about time she was coming up to say good-morning. I don't believe that you or the other members of my family would be so undutiful.

I didn't half thank you, dear pal (in words), for the trouble you took to bring me home from the yacht, and you so full of work, but I thanked you deep down, just the same; and I wanted to spare you, too, but I was born selfish, and I couldn't.

I am impatient to mail you my news. I think I will telegraph you at your New York home and try to get on your track. Meantime I am your affectionate uncle, just the same as before.

                                                              Mark

Mail-address,
John Walker, 21 Fifth Ave.
Not Clemens—they go straight to Dublin.

When Mark Twain received on September 22 a letter from a young reader about "A Dog's Tale," he sent it on to Mary Rogers in the original because, he said, "this is better than a copy would be, because the age and character show out in the handscript (as the Germans call it)." Mary Rogers might keep the letter: "Miss Lyon has kept a copy."

Dear Author

I think you are awfully mean to write such a sad terrificly sad story. I cried and cried and could not finish it.

I am going to keep the book just the same because I like you, but not as much as before (just now), but maybe I will like you more afterwards, but I really do not see how you can be quite so hard hard hearted.

With lots of thanks and No thanks at all I am

                    Your friend always,

                                                Lois Kellogg

Mark Twain meanwhile kept strenuously at work on the autobiography, "shaving 9,000 words a month," he wrote Brander Matthews early in October, into the North American Review, where it had now begun to appear as "Chapters from my Autobiography" and was to continue through twenty-five installments. There was no danger, he told Matthews, of running out of words: "There's 300,000 to draw from, not to speak of the 50,000 which I shall dictate each month until the end of time."

When he wrote his next letter to Mary Rogers, Mark Twain was in a different, less ebullient mood—at least as he started to write. By the time he had finished, he had written himself to an approximation of high spirits again. He had been to Fairhaven on another visit, and it can be suspected that something about the state of his health alarmed his hosts, so that it was Henry Rogers or his wife, or perhaps Mary Rogers herself, who sent word ahead to New York to have a physician, possibly their Dr. Edward Quintard, meet the train there on Mark Twain's arrival. His cough had been worrisome for years. It seems to have been, among other things, a smoker's cough—anyone can stop smoking, he is said to have said: I do it every day. But he was seldom without his well-caked pipe or his inexpensive and black cigars. "Most of your friends," Henry Rogers had once told him, "think that you are using your supply somewhat lavishly, but the chief complaint is in regard to the quality." And now there were increasingly troublesome pains in Mark Twain's chest, and there was shortness of breath which worried his friends. He was clearly in the doldrums when he wrote again from Dublin, beginning the letter on October 12 and finishing it five days later:

> Dublin, New Hampshire
> October 12, 1906
> Thursday, 6 p.m.

It isn't right to pelt you with a letter so soon, dear pal, but there's been a cloud-lift today and I've got to jubilate with somebody or expire with satisfaction. Next I will write Clara and between you two I expect to quiet down and become rational again.

When I was arriving from Fairhaven the physician boarded the train—he was on the watch for me—and told . . .

Here as in several places in this letter portions, indicated in our text by elipsis marks, have been snipped out roughly, as if with nail scissors. "I did not cut missing parts of this letter out," wrote Mary Rogers on the back of one of the pages. "Uncle Mark did this himself—perhaps he was sad." It can be supposed that the missing matter contained Clemens's observations, dismal, angry, or even frightened, on what the doctor had told him.

(You little rascal, if you had sent me, without waiting, the part of the letter you wrote me on the day and the night I left Fairhaven, with your victory over Harry, it would have discharged some valuable jollity into this gloom—sure!)

I will say to you and Harry (privately) that during the week that . . .

At one today I put on fresh white clothes and drove—between two very real snow-storms—to a lunch-party at the house of Professor Pumpelly—a lady-friend with much of your charm and about your age, and similarly jeweled (two little children). She has made several en

Here the letter breaks again, not deleted by cutting, but in the middle of a sentence. Mark Twain is clearly disturbed, as the next paragraph indicates.

7 p.m.

In the middle of that luncheon I got a mental-telegraphic shock, and said to myself, "Bad news is arriving at the house!"

I knew something was arriving, and most likely bad, in these days: "Twichell has fallen out of his pulpit and broken his neck—Clara has been run over by a cow—Harry has bankrupted Mary—at any rate something has gone wrong with somebody."

But it wasn't so! As soon as I was home and in bed (afternoon-habit at home but not elsewhere) Miss Lyon came up and reported. She brought your breezy and delightful letter (winner, after being so close to irremediable disaster, poor pal!) and Peterson's cablegram from Europe; and not even a rumor of trouble between Clara and the cow! Then Jean came up and sat on the bedside, and the last cloud vanished— . . .

"I will go—you are writing to Clara?"

"No, it is to my niece, my pal—stay where you are, and we will talk."

So she stayed, and was sad and subdued, but very gentle and sweet. Which wrung my heart, but threw me into a boiling internal rage—rage against brutal Nature—her half-engendered crimes against the innocent and the unoffending —for neither your sister nor Jean has done anything to deserve the afflictions visited upon them.

10 p.m.

As I had eaten luncheon I did not go to dinner, but I dressed and went down after dinner and finished reading the first half of Shakespeare's Julius Caesar aloud to Jean and Miss Lyon—that tremendous poem!—a poor enough preparation for sleep, certainly. I shall lose to-morrow; I lost to-day, and also yesterday. But it doesn't matter—there will be plenty Autobiography before we call the undertaker.

Yes, I can see the picture. I can see you quite clearly, flying around in your chaos and reducing it to order and symmetry.

Ask Harry to tie you. There is no other way to keep you from wearing yourself out. I'm glad you beat him! The fact that I am fond of him these many many years doesn't seem to keep me from rejoicing when you skin him in those contests.

Next Day, 11 a.m.—Friday

What a useful creature you are, Saccharin! When I've lost my sleep and can't dictate coherently and have to quit trying, I can turn for relief to you—I can entertain myself with scribbling incoherently to you, and you have to put up with it. Clara likewise.

Do you know, I'm practising for winter in the matter of clothes. Miss Lyon has ordered a very long grey overcoat, to hide them when I am outside—on the street. The night of the great storm I drove to the village through the deluges and talked, in the basement of the church, to a housefull of wet farmers and their families (it's a gratis monthly function instituted by the ladies of the church) all clothed in sombre colors; and my spectral costume was the only cheerful object in that place. I meant to explain my clothes, but as I was pass-ing to the platform Miss Fanny Dwight—summer-restorter, friend of ours, a person of extraordinary taste and wonderful judgment—halted me and whispered, "Mr. Clemens, you look just too sweet for anything!" I whispered back, "Miss Fanny, I was going to explain and justify these clothes, but in my opinion they don't need it now." My but some girls do have the clear eye! Isn't it so, Spontaneous C?

2 p.m.

I've lost it! What shall I do? It was more butter. But never mind, I will think it up and tell you.

I'm lying abed to-day. I dictated only ten minutes this

morning—the will wouldn't go. I'm going out to dinner. But this is a special and beloved friend—otherwise I would keep my pledge.

I'm almost afraid to send you that Westminster. But I'll do it, and you must forgive me. Which reminds me that you intimate that you came near not sending your letter, because of the pencil, etc. You mustn't even think such criminal things! No matter what you write them with—a nail, if you choose—they'll answer, don't you doubt it.

9:30 a.m., Saturday

I have been editing this letter with the scissors—for I had put into it the very dismalness which I had spared you in that recent note.

I went to that dinner-party at MacVeagh's palace last night —in white clothes. All the others—both sexes—in their noblest evening costumary. (But I know all those people familiarly.)

It is a time of surprises.

The packing suddenly began yesterday afternoon and evening, and we are to land at home in New York at 6:30 p.m. next Wednesday evening—instead of ten days later, as was the most recent previous plan. Clara will be—glad? Yes, but not entirely ready for us, perhaps. If you do not dutifully call me up, Thursday, and say good-morning, I shall be strangely tempted to call you up and scold you.

Tuesday

You hope you will come out of it "a better woman." You don't need it, Mary. You have the clean mind and the right heart, and this is a condition which is not really betterable. It is going to carry you far—out of Harry's reach and mine.

But I believe—I truly believe—we shall be allowed to call, sometimes, as the aeons drift by on their long course. St. Peter will sniff and say—

"Damn that 'mobile, throw it over the battlements!"

Angel on duty: "It isn't a 'mobile, my lord, it's brimstone. It's that over-roasted pair that come begging around, every century, smelling the place up, and—"

"What do they want?"

"To see Mary Rogers."

"Oh, we can't be always bothering with those cinders. Give them a bucket of ice and throw them over the balusters."

"But my lord, they haven't been admitted for as much as three centuries, now. It is quite pitiful. And really the old one is very nice, and he does want to see his pal very bad."

Peter (touched): "Oh, well, let him in—I remember the old wreck, and he is very nice—but heave the young one over."

"But my lord, the young one isn't so very very bad; they say there's worse ones down there."

"Oh, tell it to the marines! Still, in the circumstances— Where is Mary?"

"Thirteenth floor, your Highness."

"Jesus H! my, but she is a swell!"

"It is even so, my lord. A whole flat to herself, and doesn't associate with any but archangels."

"Ah, well, we have to strain a point for that kind. Say— does she want to see those stokers?"

"Says she does."

"Certainly there's no accounting for tastes. Send them up."

"Passenger-lift, my lord?"

"Oh, ha—a lift, no! Freight-lift, or let them climb. And say—tell them that if they ever come here again I'll heave them in amongst the Presbyterian missionaries and keep them there to all eternity!"

Take warning, Mary. If you go and play your hand for a floor or so higher, we'll never get a glimpse of you again after this life.

Your affectionate uncle,

Mark

His mood was not brightened by bad news of some kind which seems to have affected Mary Rogers. He was sympathetic but still downhearted and not at all expansive when, on October 16, he wrote the last note which survives of those he sent her from Dublin that summer.

Dublin, New Hampshire
October 16, 1906
Tuesday night

Dear Pal, there is nothing to write about but dismalness, and they would only distress you—so I will wait. I did not know it until eight this evening, when I had been in the house twenty-four hours—then I got the history of the last ten days' happenings.

I will write when there is something cheerful to say. Meantime, please dash me off a letter. Wasp, and put as many jabs and jibes and sarcasms in it as you have in stock. The more the better. Blow me a refreshing breeze!

Affectionately, your uncle,

Mark

P.S. I open this to enclose Clara's letter which has just arrived. Ordinarily—(with its sick and departing servants and its sleepless nights)—it would trouble me, but just now it is almost a gay letter, and I will send it to you to brace you up.

The letter from Clara which he forwarded must have been about her troubles in New York, where she had gone on ahead of her father to get the house ready for his return to another winter among friends there.

5

THE MAN IN THE WHITE SUIT

RETURNING himself to New York later in October, Mark Twain again took up residence at 21 Fifth Avenue. Almost every day he might be seen strolling about the neighborhood, on his way to Joe Isaacs's tobacco shop beside McClelland's tavern on Sixth Avenue or to the Brevoort Hotel where no one but Henri, the French barber, was allowed to cut Mark Twain's eye-catching white hair. Sometimes he was accompanied by old General Dan Sickles who lived across the street, but more often he was alone, walking slowly but with something of a swagger in order, he pretended to Mary Rogers, to show off his fine clothes. Since the previous summer he had dressed only in white. "I can't bear to put on black clothes again," he said: they reminded him of funerals, He envied the "beautiful rainbow hues" that women could wear. "If I should appear on Fifth Avenue on a Sunday morning clothed as I would like to be clothed, the churches would all be vacant and the congregation would come tagging after me."

Sometimes he strolled up Fifth Avenue as far as Andrew Carnegie's place at 92d Street, stopping occasionally to greet passers-by, especially young ladies or children, sometimes resting on a park bench, gesticulating with his inevitable

black cigar as he talked to some old or new-found acquaintance. Not long after his return from Dublin, he and
Henry Rogers went to the Balke-Callender Company to pick
out the billiard table Mrs. Rogers had promised him. Meanwhile he kept in his hand by playing at the Broughton's
home at 15 East 78th Street. He moved quietly back into
society, even planning to attend the wedding of Mary's friend
Sybil Kane, who was to marry young Stewart Walker at
Tuxedo Park on October 27. Henry and Mary Rogers were
spending more and more of their time at Tuxedo, and seem
not to have planned to return to their New York home on
East 57th Street until later in the season. Their activities
and Clara's occupation with her musical career had apparently kept Clara from meeting her father's young friend,
for Twain wrote:

> 21 Fifth Avenue
> Monday morning
>
> I went Sabbath-breaking to Broughton's, and beat him
> five games out of seven. Clara tried to stop me from going
> on such an errand, but I explained to her that . . . .
> She threatened to write you and ask if my explanation had
> any truth in it, but I said I wasn't afraid and dared her to go
> on. I said pals always stand by each other, right or wrong. That
> was to discourage her and it may be sufficient. And it may
> not: there is no telling. However there is no difficulty in the
> matter; if she ever brings it up, by speech or pen all you need
> to do is to say that whatever I said was true. She will believe
> you and that will put me all right and comfortable again.
>
> The fact is, I have to lead a life of chicane and deception
> with this end of the family, although it is against my nature
> and principles; and whatever help you can afford me, most

dearest pal, will be appreciated, and I will do as much for you whenever there is a chance.

(Indeed she did write you a letter, and she gave it to me to read and mail, but it seemed to me safest to suppress it—except the part wherein she said, "I was very sorry you did not come in, the day you brought my father home, and let us have the pleasure and privilege of knowing the 'Mary' he praises so much and so cordially." Clara is a dear and lovable child, but troublesome. You would like her.)

Jean departs day after tomorrow. It will add to the already sufficient solitude of this house. She doesn't go far, yet she will seem a whole light-year distant—if that isn't too extravagant a figure to use in this connection.

I am enclosing a letter from a Catholic priest. I think it's lovely. (But it's only a bait—to fish a letter out of you; we throw away most letters, but Jean wants this one; and so, it's like that pasementry gown that that charitable woman gave to the Californian sufferers and had to send for it because it belonged to another person.)

Bedad I'm going to have the privilege of attending the wedding myself! I got the invitation in Dublin—and I took it for friendly and genuine, too, not merely artificial courtesy, for I liked Miss Kane, and I noticed that if she didn't like me she didn't say so. I had a Hartford engagement, of thirty-years' standing, for the 27th, but Miss Lyon undertook to get a postponement, and she has succeeded, and now I am free. October 27th, thirty years ago, twenty or twenty-five girls of eighteen and twenty years old and thereabouts formed the Saturday Morning Club (essays and debates) and at their request I framed their rules of procedure and helped them organize. For these services they made me a member and I am a member yet—the only male one they have ever admitted. (But always when the debates began they turned me out.)

I shall see them again. How fresh and blooming and beautiful they were in that far-flown day! Some are dead now, the others are grandmothers. We've got it postponed to November 3d.

Hang those two books, they are not unpacked yet—but they will be, before long. Harry will read one of them with interest, because it is history, and is authentic; and you are to burn the other without examination.

Noon

It certainly is a vexatious world; after all this fuss and trouble and postponement it appears that I am not to get to the wedding at last, unless the impossible shall happen in my favor. But you will wish the pair prosperity and happiness for me, won't you, Mariechen?

Affectionately your uncle

Mark

It is probable that Mary Rogers was the young lady mentioned by Mark Twain in his autobiography who had earlier in the month written to him, "You are the blessedest 'accident' I have yet met with in my life." Not many days before he had talked with her about accidents, and about whether that was the proper word to use for events which to his mind were clearly part of an inevitable, inexorable series set in motion by some forgotten first cause. Fond of playing with words, she had apparently been looking for one which would describe such circumstance, for "accident," Mark Twain had told her, "is, in my belief, absolutely destitute of meaning." Whatever word she suggested in its place seems not to have pleased him when he wrote to her in a letter post-marked October 25:

> *21 Fifth Avenue*
> *October 25 1906*
> *Friday*

Mariechen dear, it must be a Latin word as it isn't in the Unabridged. The U. has only "Accipient (obsolete) a receiver."

You shouldn't come to town and not come to see a body. However, I wasn't at home to-day. I was taking exercise—on foot. Daily! I walk to the Waldorf, sit down a spell and talk to the people, then walk back to 21. To-day I meant to spread clear out to the new Piazza hotel, but at 45th Street Miss Marjorie Clinton and a young Mrs. Rogers came along in a 'mobile and gave me a lift down to Dr. Rice's, where I had an errand. I am waiting till Weston gets to Chicago, then I shall walk out to San Francisco and make him ashamed. He is vain of his age; whereas he is but a lad. I was already three years old when he was born.

Do please try to smooth it over with young Miss Walker for me; I am a little afraid to try it myself just yet. I engaged her company for the Virginia reel, then ran off to New York the day before the ball. You can tell her I had to go because I thought it was going to rain. She is very young and will not know but that it's so.

Don't you come to town again and act so.

> *Your affectionate,*
>
> Uncle Mark

Marjorie Clinton was a young neighbor of Mary's on 57th Street. Young Mrs. Rogers does not seem identifiable—she was certainly not Mary, nor could she have been her mother-in-law. Dr. Clarence C. Rice was a fashionable physician, an old friend and yachting companion, and Edward Payson Weston, who was four years younger than Mark Twain, was the celebrated veteran professional walker who at that time was on a well-publicized tramp from New York to Chicago. But, for all his getting about, Mark Twain was prey that fall to two ancient maladies, bronchitis and forgetfulness. He pled them both on November 2 in response to what must have been a teasingly scolding note from Mary Rogers:

> 21 Fifth Avenue
> November 2, 1906
> Friday morning

Can it be that I have offended you, dear pal? I do hope not. I would rather offend the Deity—twice over. Was it uncourteous in me not to write and thank you for your invitation to luncheon? I only failed of that because I have been down with bronchitis ever since Tuesday afternoon. Of course I wrote the letter, but following my habit of adding a paragraph per day, and so the book you returned has arrived before it was finished and mailed. The bronchitis assisted the delay.

But whatever my offense is, it was not intentional, and I hope not past mending, and that you will say so.

Dear me, why, I can't believe I have been guilty of anything wrong! It is unthinkable; and so I want to still sign myself your affectionate uncle

> Mark

until I am formally and officially degraded to the ranks.

Perhaps it was at this time, perhaps at another, that Mark Twain seems to have missed another appointment with Mary

and Harry Rogers. An undated letter of 1906 again presents
his apologies:

> *Saturday evening*
> *What was it that happened, dear pal? Did I make a mistake*
> *in the hour? I suppose so; I don't generally get anything right*
> *when there is a chance to get it wrong. I thought you said 10,*
> *but although I was especially and phenomenally dull-witted,*
> *Friday morning, I just had barely penetration enough to see*
> *that I had disordered your plans and Harry's; also I was sorry*
> *—not perfunctorily sorry, but really sorry—but being em-*
> *barrassed I didn't know enough to say so. So, as dulness isn't*
> *a crime, and is very very rare with me, I am fully expecting*
> *you to forgive me. O, pet of St. Peter, why didn't you tell*
> *me, you little fraud!*

November 2, however, was a day filled with excitement
for Mark Twain: the billiard table came. It was "better than
the doctors," he told Mrs. Rogers. "It is driving out the heart-
burn in a most promising way." Billiards provided wondrous
exercise: "I walk not less than ten miles every day with the
cue in my hand." The stretching and bending bring "into
play every muscle in the body. . . . If Mr. Rogers will take
daily to billiards he can do without doctors and massageurs,
I think." Each day's schedule was now reorganized: "The
games begin right after luncheon," he informed Mrs. Rogers,
"and continue until midnight, with two hours' intermission
for dinner and music." He was glad that Albert Bigelow
Paine was with him at the house, "a resident billiardist on
the premises," but the younger man was often pressed to
keep up with his employer—"nine hours' exercise per day
and ten or twelve on Sunday."

Paine remembered their games together as riotous, care-free, but very serious affairs. The new table and its pos-sibilities put immediately out of Mark Twain's head the plans which he had been making for spending part of the winter in Egypt. "I'm not going to Egypt," he told Paine after their first turn at the table. "There was a man here yesterday afternoon who said it was bad for bronchitis and, besides, it's too far from this billiard table." To Mary Rogers, four days later, he told a slightly different story, and he con-tinued to apologize for having missed her luncheon:

21 Fifth Avenue
November 7, 1906

Dear pal, there are many nieces in the world, but you are the most patient one there is, and in my opinion the only perfect one.

Yesterday morning came an invitation to Japan, for next March, and I think I came within one of persuading the Admiral to make the trip with me. But he didn't quite say yes, so I gave it up. I would like to see Japan, but the journey would be too heavy. On the 30th I made all arrangements to go to Egypt; then the bronchitis smote me, and before sunset I had canceled them all, by telegraph and telephone. There isn't any excursion I am really prepared for, except the final one; but I don't care for that one, personally, though I think St. Peter would like to see me. Let him wait; other people have to make sacrifices.

Well—yes—I was up a little late, that night, and p'raps a little weary, too, but not too weary to go to your luncheon; it was a trifle of a cold and a threat of bronchitis that lost me that pleasure and gave me a petrifying fright. Mind, I was not frightened at the thought of being killed—I don't care for being killed—but the thought of the usual six weeks in bed is a most substantial terror. But I am over that fright now, and shall soon be out on the street again. Clara keeps changing my doctors; yesterday she withdrew Halsey and called Quintard. I had a persistent and annoying dry bark for him to exploit, and he said he would send a medicine immediately that would modify it with dispatch. It didn't come. The bark continued—the rest of the day and all night. At nine this morning Clara looked in and said she had had the serenest night she had had for weeks, and it was all owing to a new medicine sent to her by Dr. Q. By the "Mr. Clemens" on the label I saw that it was my medicine, and not hers at all, and not in any way suited to her case, for she only has nervous affections, whereas I have the botts, and the heaves, and the glanders, and some other things like that. Why, Mary, I was near to death all night; at one time I did not believe I should live thirty-five years. I did not greatly mind it, on account of St. Peter perhaps waiting up for me and getting anxious, but I couldn't help wishing I could see you once more before I left. Mariechen, the more I reflect upon St. Peter and his solicitude about me, the more I like him. But formerly I didn't care for him.

I fell in love with Father Fitz Simon. The fact is I did tell him those stories, and I am ashamed; but I only did it because I thought you wouldn't hear of it. But I give you my word I won't ever do it again, I won't, indeed. It saddens me, too; for I have collected some more Don't-Marys which I would dreadfully like to tell him. And I have written a poem which is worse than the stories; and I did so want to send it to him, but I shan't because you would find it out. It was good and dear of you to apologize for me, but don't you know it's a great risk; because with your candid nature you are always sure to get in so many deleterious facts that the apology for my crime is likely to do me more damage than the crime itself.

You pay Clara a fine compliment and a true one, and then won't let me tell her? It isn't fair. Reflect—consider. Remove the prohibition.

I have dictated a while, this morning—the first time for nineteen days. On Simplified Spelling. It's good; I wish I could read it to you. Howells, Aldrich, Carnegie, and Harvey will dine here tomorrow night, and they have to listen to it. It goes to the root of the matter; proposes a reform of the idiotic alphabet. Then the orthography will reform itself. By natural compulsion, you see. I wish to God there were some more wise men in the world, I do find it so lonesome.

The new billiard table—pal, dear, you've never seen a table to approach it! You will see, when you come to try it.

Affectionately, your uncle,

Mark

P.S. My dear child, I've had an awful accident. I have coughed up my conscience. I wouldn't have taken $40 for her, she was just out of the repair shops and had fresh paint on and new rubber tyres and could go like 1830 Groombridge (see astronomy).

I am prostrated, and not able to address this note. I will ask one of the vassals to do it for me.

Dr. Robert H. Halsey and Dr. Edward Quintard were both to be increasingly in attendance during the next four years as Mark Twain's physicians. Father William Fitz-

Simon was the Episcopal rector at St. Mary's in Tuxedo Park. He seems to have been just the kind of clergyman whom Mark Twain liked best, whom he enjoyed testing, as he had so often tested his old friend the Reverend Joseph Twichell of Hartford, with earthy anecdotes designed to redden a less human and tolerant clergyman's face.

But however hearty he was in public or even in many of his letters, Mark Twain was increasingly lonely and unhappy. He was not well, and he liked the comfort of old friends around him. But they came to him now, for he went out infrequently, even turning down on November 11 an invitation for the seventieth birthday celebration for Henry Mills Alden who had sat across the table from him at the dinner to celebrate Mark Twain's arrival at what he liked to call "Pier 70" the year before. He did find time for a visit to Washington to plead for more stringent copyright regulations, and there he startled and charmed members of the Congress by appearing in white "from his feet to the crown of his silvery head," said Howells. "It was a magnificent coup, and he dearly loved a coup." Yet more and more these appearances were public gestures which tired him beyond his ability to recuperate.

He preferred to stay at home, where friends like George Harvey and Peter Finley Dunne came to match their skill with him at billiards. Henry Rogers, the "Admiral" of the *Kanawha*, also dropped in, says Paine, "with a great deal of frequency, seldom making long calls, but never seeming to have that air of being hurried which one might expect to find in a man . . . whose interests were so vast and innumerable." It was completely in accord with what seems to have been Mark Twain's most consistent mood at this

time that he should have greeted his old friend one day by
saying:

"Well, Rogers, I don't know what you will think of it, but
I think I have had about enough of this world, and I wish I
were out of it."

Henry Rogers agreed: "I don't say much about it but that
expresses my view."

Clara Clemens took abundantly good care of her father,
and during this lonely period he came to know her better and
to depend more and more on her. "She is one of the finest
and completest and most satisfactory characters I have ever
met," he told Mrs. Rogers. "Others knew it before, but I have
been busy with other matters." But Clara was not well either.
She was soon to leave for another period of rest at a
sanitarium, to build strength for a concert tour which she
planned for the beginning of the next year. On departing,
she left severe injunctions to the household at 21 Fifth
Avenue: "No billiard playing after 10 p.m." It may have been
Mark Twain's intention to ignore her restriction which kept
Clara now guiltily on her father's conscience. The sketch
which he made of himself, to be included with his Christmas
gift to her, seems only to survive in the description of it
which he wrote to Mary Rogers on November 19:

> *21 Fifth Avenue*
> *November 19, 1906*
> *Monday a.m.*

Hang it! . . .
No, that doesn't sound right. . . .
It must be dang it. . . .
But I don't feel certain. Which do you think is right, Mary?
which do you prefer? which one do you use?

I have forgotten what I was going to say, but it is no matter. I am only writing this note—this half note in order to enclose this latest, and get your opinion of it. It is for a locket for Clara, and is to be a Xmas surprise. To me it seems excellent and full of delicate feeling, and sweetness and joy. And I think there is a deep earnestness and conviction about the expression which is most impressive. The ears are not the same but that is because they are rights and lefts. On my father's side of the house we have always worn them so. It is very becoming, I think. This portrait looks too holy perhaps —holier than is my custom to look, except on the Sabbath— but it is because of the new way I dressed my hair for the sitting.

I am finishing a remarkable book, dear pal, by a child of fifteen. You will have seen reviews of it. It is virile and rugged and will make a pleasant change for you after the polished diction of The Call of the Blood. Will you be good and come and get it, or shall you prefer that I send it to you. (If I may have a choice, it's the former.) When is your next singing lesson? Won't you call me on the telephone? I expect to be permitted to step outside the house about January or February.

This isn't good weather, Mary dear; it makes me feel mouldy.

Affectionately, your uncle,

Mark

Miss Lyon has been ill in bed a week, and it seemed as if I never could begin the burden of clearing off the accumulated mail. But at last I went at it with determination last night and accomplished it in five minutes without a penstroke. By help of the fire. It shows what native talent, unobstructed by principle, can do, when duty calls.

A few days later, the ailing Miss Lyon went to Hartford for a rest. The next day she wrote her employer: "I was unhappy to have to go away yesterday without the chance of having you speak to me; but the human race was getting it, for you were saying that the human race was a disappointment, and no better—or not as good as—the monkey. I went down the front steps feeling like a monkey—a sorry monkey, and by his looks you know how sorry a monkey can feel."

Her letter seemed so delicious that Mark Twain sent it on to Mary Rogers, adding this in explanation:

> 21 Fifth Avenue
>
> *I was dictating in the front room, ground floor, when she passed out to take her train. She heard only the opening sentence: "I believe that our Heavenly Father invented man because he was disappointed in the monkey." I have told the stenographer to write and tell her she only heard the gentlest sentences in the whole chapter—wait and see the rest.*
>
> *You see, I didn't know anybody was overhearing me. I don't mind Miss Lyon, but it might have been you, and it might have been Clara: I don't want either of you around, except when I'm concealing my real opinions. There's no considerable liberty possible, when there's a niece or a daughter on the bridge.*
>
> *At this very moment I am only waiting for Clara to depart for her train, then I am going to get up and do some forbidden things and have a pleasant time.*
>
> 10 minutes later
>
> *She has come and she has gone. I shall have adventures now.*

The book by a fifteen-year-old girl which Mark Twain recommended to Mary Rogers was probably *The Viper of Milan: A Romance of Lombardy* by Gabrielle Margaret Vere Campbell, a young Scottish girl whom he seems to have met in Paris or London where she was studying art, and who wrote then and continues to write over the pseudonym of Marjorie Bowen. Most accounts state that this, her first novel, was published when she was sixteen—it may have been that in making her a year younger Mark Twain had in mind her age when the book was written. Miss Bowen's romance would, he thought, provide an antidote for Robert Hichens's sensational *The Call of the Blood* which was then running as a serial in *Harper's Bazaar*.

He was to recommend other books to Mary also, and to send her some, presumably of his own. One of them was a "dreadful book" which he hoped she would not read. But she did, and, Mark Twain said in his next letter, he was not sorry. People had strange notions of what was and what was not proper. Little had been made in the newspapers about the banning of *Eve's Diary* by a provincial library because its illustrations pictured Adam and Eve without clothing, but the incident bothered Mark Twain. When reporters approached him for comment, he explained, "I believe this time the trouble is mainly with the pictures. I did not draw them. I wish I had—they are so beautiful." Writing to another friend, he said, "When a library expels a book of mine and leaves an unexpurgated Bible lying around where unprotected youth can get ahold of it, the deep unconscious irony of it delights me." To Mary Rogers, he wrote on November 28 of these and other things, apparently forgetting that he had spoken of some of them before:

21 *Fifth Avenue*
November 28, 1906
Monday

Dear pal, you have a very accurate instinct: I had been in mischief—which isn't unusual, even with me—and I was a little afraid to tell you the details. I still think that the crimes I had been committing in your absence will fare better unconfessed, though really I can give you my word they were no worse than usual.

I am not sorry you have read that dreadful book, but my main idea was to have Harry read it; because it is history and in the line of his literary likes and interests. But my! its horrors are the merest trifles compared with King Leopold's bloody doings in the Congo State to-day. I have been arranging for Leopold with St. Peter. Also I got a contract out of him for weather for you, and for the babies. If the weather furnished is not satisfactory, let me know. Peter has promised to advance you a story higher. I asked him to give Harry and me a lift, too, but he murmured as if to himself "in my father's house are many flats, but we don't need any more just now." Do you think he meant Harry? He wouldn't mean both of us, would he, do you think? Would it be courteous—with me right there? He was a little reserved with me, because he had heard about the Charlton library banishing Eve's Diary on account of the pictures, and hadn't yet made up his mind what stand he would take in the matter. He was very much interested in the pictures, and was taking as suspiciously long a time examining them as had that clothed but unclean-minded librarianess. Seven interviewers have been here, but I have not seen them, and have been careful to send them word that I could not talk upon the matter because I felt no

interest in it—which is true; but in one case I forgot myself
and said a bright thing. But no harm has come of it. The
newspaper doubted the commercial wisdom of printing it, I
judge.

Clara's just gone! ordered to the country for two months
by the doctor. She wouldn't consent to go until I made a lot
of promises. I mean to keep some of them. But I was to begin
last night and I didn't. I caught a fresh cold in the billiard
room and had a horrible night. I was outside the house
twenty minutes yesterday, for the first time in several weeks.
I was to repeat, to-day—by command—but

This is the House of Gayety! Miss Lyon left for Hartford
day before yesterday—ordered by the doctor to remain away
and rest two weeks. Jean's gone, Clara's gone—there'll be
nobody on the premises but the servants and me for a fort-
night. And it is a week of anniversaries—this one—and there
is nothing else that is so hard to get through with. They are
the birth anniversaries of two of my dead, and of my own
birth—and—worst of all—Thanksgiving Day. Not the dinners
—they are pleasant—but the rest of the day, with its cloud of
reminiscences and its dim procession of passing spectres.

3 p.m.

Last year I was loaded to the eyebrows with public engagements, from October 23 till mid-April. This year I have declined every public invitation, except one. I accepted that one
day before yesterday, and have canceled it to-day. Mary, there
are few people who are wiser than I—indeed I don't suppose
there are any. I wish I could have been born the same day
with Solomon; just to see if he would still be remembered
now.

"Du bist wie eine Blume"—and the rest of it. It all applies to you, dear niece.

Affectionately, your uncle,

Mark

Some part of Christmas Day in 1906 seems to have been spent happily with the Rogerses, and Mary gave her Uncle Mark a picture. It can be assumed from the following letter, written on the next day, that the mysterious telephone message of which it speaks provided its share to the conversation. But much of it must have been concerned with the trip to Bermuda which the Rogers family thought would be beneficial for Mark Twain, now when New York was getting colder and Bermuda was sunny and warm.

21 Fifth Avenue
December 26, 1906
10:30 a.m.

Mariechen dear, the mystery came very near to a solution, yesterday afternoon. I stated the problem to Miss Lyon, and after she had thought it over a few minutes, she said,

"It must have been Mrs. Rogers, the mother of Francis Rogers the baritone—she and Clara are warm friends."

But when Clara arrived at 10 yesterday from visiting Jean, she said,

"No, the Mrs. Rogers of the mystery said, 'Tell your father we have returned to town.' She wouldn't be sending messages to you, for she is not acquainted with you."

Clara thinks it must have been some friend of hers whose name was made to seem Rogers by a defective telephone. However, the final telephonic remark to Clara was, "After a day or two, let us arrange an appointment."

Very well, there'll be another telephonic message from the mystery, you see—then Clara will get her name.

Naturally I came home yesterday almost entirely convinced that Bermuda-in-summer and suicide are interchangeable terms. By midnight I had almost come to the conclusion to retire from the experiment.

Then I thought I would talk about it and be guided by his advice. So I went there, and crept into his bosom, stirred him out of his dreams, and stated my case. He said,

"Who was it that said it was a bad summer climate?"

"Oh, Broughton, Coe, the Admiral—in fact all the family."

"And your niece?"

"Yes."

"What do they know about it?"

"They don't know. But they have heard."

"Heard?"

"Yes."

"What kind of evidence is heard?"

"I—well, I dunno."

* * * (Reflection.)

"When were you here last?"

"A little over three centuries ago."

"How did you find my bosom then—considered as a climate?"

"Well—er—"

"Oh, speak out!"

"Well, it was pretty damp and sweltry."

"But on the whole, comfortable?"

"Y—e—s—oh, quite."

"You had just come from visiting your Uncle Harry. How was his place for climate?"

"Oh, insufferably warm and dry!"

"Now then, how should you regard an average between my climate and his'n?"

"Oh, prime—just the thing!"

"All right—that is actually what Bermuda in summer is. With this advantage—that there you have sweet sea-breezes. It wouldn't answer for your niece, I grant you that. She is young, and unseasoned. But you are old and mouldy and seasoned. Ask Peter about her—he knows. Take my advice: try Bermuda."

So that settled it, and made me once more anxious to make the experiment.

11:45

Twichell is ready to go—as per letter just received.

11:50

Miss Lyon has telephoned Will Coe, and he is securing the passages for Jan. 2.

It is time to get up.

Many many many thanks for the picture, Mary dear—it is excellent.

Your affectionate uncle,

Mark

New Year's Eve at 21 Fifth Avenue was gay with story-telling, charades, and music. Mark Twain, pretending to be a baby, acted out the word "pain." He and Witter Bynner together played the part of Siamese twins, miming the word "champagne"—"I getting drunk," Mark Twain wrote to Jean, "on wine drunk by him." But the feature of the evening, at five minutes before midnight, was a demonstration of the telharmonium: "lovely music—played on a silent piano of 300 keys at the corner of Broadway a mile and a half away, and sent over telephone wires to our parlor—the first time this marvelous invention ever uttered its voice in a private house." Mark Twain was in high good spirits. He told his guests how he had been the first author to use a typewriter, how he had been among the first of any men to use a fountain pen, and how his was the first telephone installed in a private house—and now the telharmonium: within a year or two, he said, music like this would go to thousands of homes, as "cheap as water . . . and you can shut it off when you please, like the gas." The company left at one, "and Mr. Paine and I played billiards till 3 o'clock," he confessed to Jean. "I am tired."

The next day the Reverend Joseph Twichell arrived from Hartford, and the day after he and Mark Twain, with Miss Lyon to watch over them, were bundled off to Bermuda, to stay a week.

6

BUTTER WANTED

WHEN spring came, Mark Twain rented a house, apparently from the William Vosses, in Tuxedo Park and not far from Harry and Mary Rogers. Tuxedo seemed to him, he wrote Henry Rogers, "a charming place; I think it hasn't its equal anywhere." It was probably not long after his arrival that he sent the following invitation to his young friends:

The pleasure of the company of
Mr. and Mrs. H. H. Rogers, Jr.
is requested at the Voss domicile on Wednesday 1:30 p.m.
to meet Mr. Clemens, the celebrated humorist.
Informal.
Dress not necessary.
Only clothes.

Mary Rogers's sister Frances was to be married to Edgar Lackland of St. Louis at the Rogerses' Tuxedo home in May, and Mark Twain grieved that he could not be there. The wedding was to be one of the events of the season. The Reverend Percy Stickney Grant was coming from New York to perform the ceremony, and all of society would be there.

21 Fifth Avenue

To the Shah-in-Shah of Nieces—

Greetings and salutation:

Oh dear me! that I should have this ill luck—the only member of the family that can't be there. For I shall be in Maryland then, and shan't get back to Tuxedo until next Monday or Tuesday. I am sorry and disappointed; for I was counting on the pleasure of being present. Yes, and I was going to scrape acquaintance with Mr. Lackland on the basis of the fact that I knew a Lackland in St. Louis forty-seven years ago in the steamboat trade. Not that I knew him well, but only as a subordinate knows a superior, his rank being so much higher than mine to forbid a nearer connection. I tell you, etiquette was strict out there, Mary dear! Do please convey for me my cordial congratulations to the bride and groom.

When you are out driving, won't you call at my house and get a novel (published by McClure) by Marjorie Bowen, and read a part or all of it and tell me what you think of it? Please. I don't remember its name, but it is the only one by M. B. You can read it without prejudice or predilection, but I couldn't, because it is dedicated to me. It is based on the Massacre of Glencoe, but it mercifully leaves out (or very gently touches) the main horrors. I think that it is greatly to the girl's credit, for there would naturally be a strong temptation to do the other thing.

The Fair started well, this afternoon, and I am sure it is going to be handsomely successful. It would have interested you, and I was sorry you were not there.

If you will be so good, dear madam, as to present my humble service to your estimable daughter, and say that the tenderness which I—but of this anon.

Affectionately, your uncle,

Mark

I am glad you sent the note by Harry, because all letters for 21 Fifth Avenue not addressed to "Mr. John Walker" are turned back at the Post Office and go to Tuxedo.

The Fair which Mark Twain mentioned may have been held in connection with the Jewish Educational Alliance of New York, whose Children's Theater that fall put on a production of *The Prince and the Pauper*. Or it may have been a simple local affair held at Tuxedo Park. The book by Marjorie Bowen which he recommended to Mary Rogers was *The Master of the Stair* which had been published in April, dedicated "To Mark Twain with deep gratitude for the flattering interest shown by a great man of letters in the work of a beginner." He was wrong in describing it as the only book by Marjorie Bowen—he had already apparently recommended her first book, *The Viper of Milan*, to Mary Rogers some months before. Perhaps he simply meant that it was the only book by Marjorie Bowen in his house at that time.

Meanwhile work on the house which John Mead Howells had designed for him near Redding in Connecticut had begun. "I have signed the contract," Mark Twain wrote to Henry Rogers, "and specified the cost limit." It was to be paid for complete by the proceeds of "a year's installments of the Autobiography" in the *North American Review*: he still thought he might call it Autobiography House. Everything seemed to be moving along more happily now. Jean was being cared for in a home nearby, and Clara, said her father, "is winning her way to success and distinction with sure and steady strides. By all accounts she is singing like a bird." Early in May the newspapers announced that Mark Twain would go to England, to receive there an honorary degree from Oxford. He came down to New York to get ready. The house at 21 Fifth Avenue was a bustle of preparation.

He sailed from New York on June 8, 1907, with an ad-monitory "dusting off" note from Clara in his pocket. She gave him, he explained to shipmates, "instructions how to act on every occasion": if he obeyed them all, he would be more celebrated in England for his behavior than for any-thing else. His daughter had particularly insisted that he was to appear properly clothed, not always in white. But the injunction was too severe, and he decided to disregard it. As he shuffled about the deck of the *Minneapolis*, he seems to have been the pet of every passenger, especially of the younger ones, and most especially of the younger ones when they were girls. "I had reached the grandfather stage of life without grandchildren," he explained, "so I began to adopt some." He growled at them from behind his moustaches like a friendly lion, he played games with them, and he told stories incessantly.

England greeted him with warm enthusiasm. He attended the King's garden-party at Windsor Castle, breakfasted with Lord Avebury, lunched with Bernard Shaw, dined with Lord and Lady Portsmouth, and called on Mr. and Mrs. Rogers who were staying briefly at Claridge's Hotel. He was a man, said Augustine Birrell, whom Englishmen and Americans do well to honor, for his humor has joined the English-speaking world in a brotherhood of laughter. "England has had a glorious week with Mark Twain," wrote a commentator for *Harper's Weekly.* "His humor has never been happier nor his zest in life more abounding."

At Oxford on June 26 he received his degree side by side with Rudyard Kipling, Auguste Rodin, Camille Saint-Saëns, General William Booth of the Salvation Army, and his old friend Prime Minister Campbell-Bannerman to whom he had written humorous congratulations not a year before. "Most amiable and charming sir," said Lord Curzon, as Chancellor of the University, when he conferred Mark Twain's degree, "you shake the sides of the world with your merriment." The words were said in Latin, which Mark Twain could only pretend to understand, but as he stood there with his great shock of white hair seeming the whiter because of the brilliance of his scarlet academic gown, and as the undergraduates cheered and hooted and threw their caps—"If only Tom Sawyer could have seen him then!" said Albert Bigelow Paine. "If only Olivia Clemens could have sat among those who gave him welcome."

He remained in England for a little more than two weeks after the ceremony, feted wherever he went, seeing old friends. The round of dinners and entertainments was enervating, but, he told Henry Rogers, "I do very much want to meet up with the boys for the last time."

Returning to Tuxedo Park late in July, he resumed his quiet routine of dictation and mild social pleasures. He would have liked to visit with the Rogerses at Fairhaven that fall, but, explained Miss Lyon, "he has been very much tied up here, trying to finish his dictation of the trip to England. If he stops once to go away for a day or so, he says he knows he will be unable to resume work again and so he dares not break in on what he feels is a very great duty. He has been working very steadily; in fact," she wrote on August 27, "today he has done too much and has gone to bed very tired."

He was worried now about plans for celebration of Robert Fulton Day at the Jamestown Exposition in Virginia. Because 1907 was the centennial of the invention of the steamboat, the Robert Fulton Memorial Association planned an impressive, ceremonial gathering in the giant auditorium at Jamestown. Though the roster of the association was crammed with prominent names—Cornelius Vanderbilt was its president; John Jacob Astor, Andrew Carnegie, Nicholas Murray Butler, and Cleveland Dodge were members of its executive committee—much of the work in getting together a memorial program seemed to rest on the shoulders of its vice-president, Samuel L. Clemens.

Only one thing seemed certain, that he would be able to make the trip to Jamestown on Henry Rogers's *Kanawha*, and that Harry and Mary Rogers would go along with him. But the arrangements, the finding of a speaker—these things gave him great trouble. It had seemed possible that the Hon. Joseph H. Choate might come over from Europe for the occasion, but he wrote from The Hague that his work there made the trip impossible. Nicholas Murray Butler of Columbia was considered as an alternate, but that failed to work out either. Mark Twain was ready to throw over the whole affair. "What with doing a heavy day's work, and with fretting over the complications of securing the right orator for the Fulton Memorial Day at Jamestown," said his secretary, "he is very tired." He had her telephone Jamestown to inform the people there that "Mr. Clemens now felt that he could withdraw and take no further part in the celebration." But, Miss Lyon reported to Mrs. Rogers, "it seems they count so much on having Mr. Clemens there; they feel so that without him they might as well give up all idea of having a celebration, as he is their great card, and their disappointment is so keen that Mr. Clemens will reconsider his decision to withdraw." Mark Twain himself wrote to Henry Rogers: "We shall hurry through at Jamestown as quickly as possible, so that we can return the yacht to you." Mary Rogers thought they might start toward home at midnight, after the celebrations were over—"so that," said her Uncle Mark, "is what we shall do."

On September 23 the *Kanawha*, which the official *Blue Book* of the Exposition described as "in charge of Dr. Samuel L. Clemens who had with him several distinguished guests," joined a three-mile parade of vessels, large and small, which streamed into Hampton Roads in honor of Robert Fulton. A gale was blowing and the going ashore by launch was perilous especially for the ladies dressed and beribboned as representatives of various patriotic organizations. "It was the completest and perfectest fiasco in history," said Mark Twain, "and worth going a thousand miles to see." But, he said, Harry and Mary Rogers "saved the day for me." As your deputies, he told Henry Rogers, "they very much exceeded the due hospitalities devolved upon them by their official position. It would have been no breach of hospitality if they had remained on board that stormy 23d, but they didn't; they saw me ashore themselves. It was a shame to allow them to do it—I realized that—but I hadn't the grit to 'stay aboard,' for the R. F. day was bound to be a failure and a fiasco, and I greatly needed the countenance and presence and support of friends, otherwise my share of the fiasco could easily be disastrous."

When Mark Twain, all in white, even to necktie and shoes, entered the auditorium, the great crowd gathered there "arose and cheered while the distinguished humorist marched to the stage," reported the official proceedings of the occasion. "Certainly no Exposition visitor had received such a welcome, and Mr. Clemens, though accustomed to enthusiastic greetings, was visibly touched. For almost a moment after the applause ceased, he tried to speak and the audience rightly estimating the reasons for his hesitation, again began to cheer."

Ostensibly, Mark Twain was only to introduce Rear Admiral P. F. Harrington, who was to speak as representative of the nautical professions, before the Hon. Martin W. Littlefield—whom Mark Twain had not known before and was delighted to learn was his neighbor on Fifth Avenue and also an avid billiard player—was to "hold the audience spellbound for nearly an hour." But Mark Twain was the drawing card, and he, and everyone else, knew it. He told his audience that the application of steam to sea navigation was peculiarly an American event, and deserved national commemoration. There were not, he said, many genuine American holidays, not even the Fourth of July. All the great events which led up to that day were made by English subjects, not by Americans; subjects of the King did virtually all of the fighting, on both sides. But "it was an American who applied steam successfully. There are not many great world events, but we have our own full share. The telegraph, the telephone, and the application of steam navigation are American."

He pretended then that he and Admiral Harrington had been present when Fulton first steamed up the Hudson. In fact, he explained, "the Admiral and myself have held public office and have also been together a great deal in a friendly way since the time of Pocahontas. The incident when Pocahontas saves the life of Smith from her father, Powhatan's club, was gotten up by the Admiral and myself to advertise

Jamestown." He turned serious for a minute to commend Admiral Harrington's public service, but ended with a characteristic Mark Twain peroration, spoken straight-faced and slowly, with the beetling of his brows hiding any twinkle which might have been in his eyes as he spoke: "I will say that the same high qualities, the same moral and intellectual attainments, the same graciousness of manner, of conduct, of observation and expression have caused Admiral Harrington to be mistaken for me and I have been mistaken for him."

The crowd roared with laughter and cheered long, but Mark Twain was tired. That evening at the official dinner of the Association he was almost pathetically buoyed up to see Harry and Mary Rogers among the guests. "I had not dreamed that they would take all that trouble and come back, after all the trouble they had taken to help me through the day." He was grateful to them, he pretended to Henry Rogers, because "their presence forbade me to shame them with certain vicious and ungracious public utterances which longed for an outlet, but which were better unsaid than said. I was discrete and proper and parliamentary, but the credit was not mine."

Later that fall a light-hearted correspondence was carried on between Mark Twain, back in Tuxedo Park, and the Rogerses in Fairhaven. Playing again on the old theme of Mark Twain's inordinate desire for compliments and at the old game of long words, he wrote to Mary Rogers:

BUTTER WANTED
Any Kind:
New; Old;
Salted; Unsalted;
Odorless; Fragrant;

Real preferred, but
Oleomargarine not turned away.
Apply at the old stand,
21 Fifth Ave.,
at the
Sign of the Butterfly.

O Arisodactylous was his name,
And dactylous [was] his [nature] morals
Holopothal his [moral] [holy] constant state
[And given o'er to] Diversified by quarrels

Corrected Form

O Arisodactylous was his name,
And dactylous his morals,
Holopothal his constant state,
Diversified by quarrels.

To be continued by the Shah-in-Shah (Anglice, The Pal of Pals) at her convenience.

P.S. I seem to be always asking favors of you—still I have to ask one more: Won't you please try Mr. Paine's Christian Scientist? he cured Paine's agonizing headaches permanently, after years of torture. He has helped some kind of an ailment of Clara's, and has greatly modified Miss Lyon's chronic and dreadful headaches—not personally but through Paine. He will do you no harm, Mariechen, if he does you no good. You may gain, and you can't lose. Will you try him? Say you will. Put aside prejudice—prejudice is nobody's sure friend.

P.P.S. That same man restored John Howells to good and sound health when he had long been a wreck and just a museum of pestilent maladies. *John doesn't like this to be known, but he confesses the truth of it.*

Monday, 10:50 a.m.

Tuxedo Club,

Tuxedo Park

New York

(really, New Jersey, I guess.)

It's a pleasant sound, that voice of yours, dear pal.

THE END

The Rogerses invited Mark Twain to Fairhaven, but he seems to have been too occupied with other things, probably with continued dictation, for he felt increasingly that he had much to say and not much time to say it in. But he exchanged sportive postcards with them which have not survived, so that their contents can only be imagined from what he or Mary Rogers wrote about them. It was probably during the first week in October that he wrote to her:

Read this and grit your teeth, Mariechen dear. Yesterday you were sending me that cunning post-card picture of a brother of mine, with the unrighteous purpose of "taking me down a peg"—as you slangers phrase it—and this morning comes this nice buttery card from a just and judicious shipmatess, and antidotally sets my self-complacency up again, a whole peg higher than it was before! Grit your teeth & try again—maybe you'll score next time. Henry will sail at 10 tomorrow, and I am tied up and out of luck.

With love,

Uncle Mark

She replied to him on October 7, repeating the family's invitation for a visit:

October 7, 1907

Dear Uncle Mark,

Father Rogers has asked me to return your scurrilous literature, and to say, that as for him, he will have nothing to do with persons who indulge in anonymous postcards, however much he might feel himself in sympathy with their sentiments.

He hopes that having enjoyed yourself, by taking away your own character, so openly you are ready to suffer the penalty, with meekness, which the law inflicts on those who are caught sending opprobrious remarks through the mail.

Only an arisodactyl Hellenist would behave so rudely.

Your most affectionate Niece

Mary

(Meaning more affectionate than your other nieces.)

Father Rogers says the aforementioned "penalty" is waiting you down here and he wants you to come and get it.

A day later, on October 8, probably before he had received Mary's letter, Mark Twain wrote to her father-in-law that he would come to Fairhaven at the end of that week, by the New Bedford boat or, he suggested, the *Kanawha*. Then he reverted to the postcard game:

Oh well, there's different kinds of postcards, they're not all like the one you sent, thanks be! Mary wrote that one. I recognized her hand through the disguise, without any trouble. Another thing: you told her to return my scurrilous literature, along with your indignation. Very well, she sent the indignation, but kept the literature for her scrap book.

*I knew she would admire it. I will ask you to give me her
love, and thereto my thanks for her appreciation of that
literature. And it is good, you know, very good.*

But as the postscript to the following letter written from
Tuxedo Park on October 11 indicates, he was too late. The
whole Rogers clan was returning to New York.

Tuxedo Park
October 11, 1907

*Mariechen dear, Flower of Nieces, it was my purpose to
thank you for your letter in person, but the court had a
more different idea about it, and it forbade Fairhaven, and
furnished me a couple of day's testifying to do.*

*Ah, you ought to see the baby! I have seen the baby. It is
beautiful, but not so beautiful as the mother. It looks wonderfully young, but that is a Kane specialty, they all look that
way. I did not get its good opinion, but that was my own
fault. It overheard me say it looked like Bryan. I meant it as
a compliment, but I would have chosen some one else if I
had known it was prejudiced. I am always doing the unfor-
tunate thing, and always meaning the opposite. The child did
not say anything, but I know by its expression that the next
time I call I shall not get in. Yet I give you my word of
honor, I wouldn't have wounded it for anything in the world.
I want to write it a letter, if you think that that would do
any good.*

*I walked every step of the way out there and back, except
that a lady carried me up the hill in her brougham and left
me at the door. I mean to take a walk every year—it does me
good. Down in the road, coming away, I met Grandmother*

Van der Weyde

Mark Twain wrote
Mary that he
was holding a
letter from her
in his hand
when he posed
for this picture.

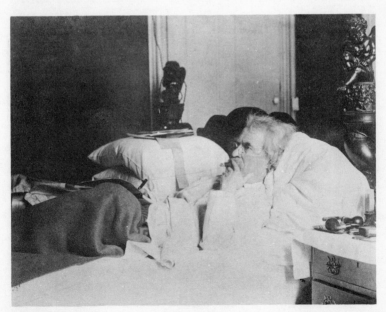

Brown Brothers, N.Y.

During these later years, Mark Twain did much of his writing
comfortably propped up in bed.

The man in the white suit on the doorstep of his Tuxedo Park home.

The new billiard table. Mark Twain and Albert Bigelow Paine are engaged in an unorthodox maneuver.

Kane, looking as girlish and handsome as ever, and with her
was another girl, her daughter.

You will find your sloping lawn satisfactorily green and
comely, when you arrive; and there's a fine crop of tall yellow
flowers down by the water—crocuses, I reckon.

I don't know what the penalty is that's hanging over me,
but I know the anfractuosities of the Admiral's temper well
enough to know that he will forget all about it before he gets
a chance to inflict it.

Come along home, please.

To my most affectionate niece—these, from her most
affectionate

Uncle Mark

P.S. 5 p.m. Telegram from Mrs. Broughton, Great Neck:

"The yacht left for Fairhaven to-day to bring all the family
home on Sunday."

Including you and your triplets, I hope. Instead of burning
this I will allow myself the privilege of mailing it to your
home here as a Welcome.

The baby whom Mark Twain mentioned must have belonged to Sybil and Stewart Walker whose wedding he had
attended, or planned to attend, the year before. "Triplets"
must have referred to Mary's two children and her young
husband. Mary Rogers continued to tease her Uncle Mark.
He had returned to New York for the winter and resumed
his rambling jaunts up Fifth Avenue, susceptible still to
the lure of a lift part of the way by some young lady in an
automobile. Mary had seen him at it, she said, in someone
else's car. He denied it in a letter dated November 21, and
denied also that he had failed to attend the wedding of their

friend Clarence Rice the month before. Who "Coontz" was is not easily established—perhaps it was a private name for her husband Harry.

21 Fifth Avenue
November 21, 1907

Well, dear, you are a brilliant little rascal, and the flashes spurt up all along your sentence-wires, interval by interval, and if I had a mile-perspective on them I should think it was a trolley, blue-sparking its way down the distances—but

You haven't any principles and I was never able to teach you any; and so you'd druther tell me what ain't so than what is. I haven't been mobiling at all. And besides it wasn't a mile, it was only a quarter of a mile; and you were not paddling alongside, for a mile, nor a quarter of a mile, nor for even three yards—for you couldn't come within three yards of me, in dark or daytime and I not know it—and so, those two foundationless statements of yours are blown to Uranus; and besides she was not in the mobile, and I was not saying anything to her anyway except—at any rate nothing that would instruct you any, since there wasn't a word nor an art that I hadn't learned of you, you small humbug, at Jamestown on Coontz's Day. And you?—why didn't you hail me? You would if I had been there, and you would anyway, if you had been there yourself.

And as for the Rice wedding, I was there. But you were not, or I should have seen you. I entered with St. Clair McKelway's wife, and sat down in a corner, close by a side-door—port side, as you enter. I saw everybody that entered by that orifice, and you were not among them. There, now—all your statements have fallen by the wayside like the tares that were sown in Sodom and Gomorrah by David and Goliath and took not root because the ram's horns of Jericho blew them on the wings of the morning to the uttermost parts of the sea. Mary dear, dear sweet niece—reform! I will help you.

Didn't I tell you not to come to town again without calling on me? Haven't I any authority at all? Why didn't you come and take me mobiling? But I know—it was because Coontz was around, and you could do better. I think it's scandalous!

November 29

Mariechen, I didn't say sins. I said it covered a multitude of charms. And it is perfectly true. I wish you wouldn't be always misquoting me and discouraging all my attempts to learn how to be veracious. For I do so want to learn how, dear.

I don't know where you are but I am guessing that you are in Tuxedo. You were very delightful yesterday.

Affectionately, your uncle,

Mark

There seems to be no question that Mark Twain enjoyed the company of ladies, of whatever age. Perhaps it would be more correct to say that he simply liked company, and that he liked best to pick his own company. Certainly he was lonely. That winter brought the usual round of dining out, of banquets and ceremonial meetings, and "these things," he admitted, "furnished me intellectual cheer and entertainment, but they got into my heart for an evening only, then left it dry and dusty." Better were the meetings of the Human Race Club, composed of old friends like Colonel Harvey, William Dean Howells, Peter Finley Dunne, and Henry Rogers, who met, or who were supposed to meet irregularly at 21 Fifth Avenue for cigars and leisurely talk. But these were all busy men, hard to get together. So Mark Twain inaugurated that winter a series of "doe" luncheons to which ladies only were invited and at which he presided proudly as the only male. They were "pretty affairs," said Albert Bigelow Paine. Clara Clemens acted as hostess. Geraldine Farrar came, and Mrs. Frank Doubleday, Mrs. Robert Collier, and Kate Douglas Riggs who asked one day whether, if being invited to one luncheon made her a "doe," being invited to two would make her a "doe-doe." "I cannot report these luncheons," said Paine, "for I was not present, and the drift of the proceedings came to me later in too fragmentary a form to be used as history; but I gathered from Clemens that he had done all the talking." On February 7, 1908, Mark Twain invited Mary Rogers to join the select company:

> 21 *Fifth Avenue*
> *February* 7, 1908

> *Tuesday*
> *Feb.* 11
> 1 *p.m.*
> *Doe-Luncheon*
> *above address.*
> *Mind you don't forget it, Mariechen dear.*
> *Your affectionate*
> *Uncle Mark*

On February 22 he joined Henry Rogers, whose health at that time worried his family, on an extended visit to Bermuda. As they stood on the pier surrounded by reporters who had come to see them off, Mark Twain pretended concern because he had not quite enough money for a round trip ticket. Henry Rogers joined in the pleasantries by suggesting that his companion sell jokes to the reporters at one dollar each until the balance was made up. Mark Twain regarded him sternly as he explained that his purpose in going to Bermuda was to keep Mr. Rogers straight.

The holiday seems to have been good for them both. As they rode about the island, they were pointed to affectionately as the King and the Rajah. "There was generally a group to gather around them," said Paine, "and Clemens was sure of an attentive audience, whether he wanted to air his philosophies, his views on the human race, or to read aloud from the verses of Kipling." To Mrs. Rogers Mark Twain wrote of her husband: "He is getting along splendidly! This is the very place for him. He enjoys himself and is quarrelsome as a cat."

7

STORMFIELD AND AFTER

MARK TWAIN made only a few public appearances during the spring of 1908. He and Henry Rogers went together one afternoon to the Aldine Club where with John D. Rockefeller they confronted and charmed a company of magazine publishers among whom, Mark Twain said, there was probably not one who had not been in the habit during the past several years of abusing the chiefs of the Standard Oil Company. He addressed a booksellers' banquet, graciously but humorously confessing his debt, of various kinds, to those who had helped promote his career as an author. In May he took part in dedication ceremonies for the new site of the College of the City of New York, and he spoke at Delmonico's on Queen Victoria's birthday.

By June the new house in Connecticut was ready for occupancy. Mark Twain had not seen it, nor had he cared to. All plans, even to landscaping and decoration, had been left to young Howells and Clara, with capable and devoted assistance from Miss Lyon. The owner's only stipulation had been that the billiard room must be done in red—all his billiard rooms had been red, and he wanted no change. He knew in a general way that the house stood on a hill, and that it was

large, built on the model of an Italian villa. By the middle
of the month the house at 21 Fifth Avenue was again in a
bustle of preparation for this final move. Three days before
he left New York, Mark Twain wrote Mary Rogers on
June 15:

> 21 Fifth Avenue
> June 15, 1908
> Monday

*Mariechen dear, it is lovely of you to invite me, and I do wish
I could say yes, but am tied up with preventive engagements
—that is to say, company at "Innocence at Home" (name of
the house I have built in the country—you are permitted to
keep your sarcasms to yourself, dear; and it wouldn't be safe
for you to utter any, anyway.)*

*The final last tinkering and fussing and finishing was com-
pleted yesterday—the Sabbath day, and everything is ship-
shape and ready now. Miss Lyon and the servants and the
four cats will go up tomorrow morning and take possession,
and I am to follow two days later, in the late afternoon.
Friends will arrive Friday, Saturday and Monday. I am con-
scious of a steadily augmenting great curiosity to see what the
house looks like. And also the region round about. Clara and
Miss Lyon claim that it is as beautiful as Tuxedo, but I doubt
it.*

*Of course you can have any head I've got, and right wel-
come—but I don't know of any "large" head, unless you
mean the brown-tinted London one such as H. H. has. If
that is it, I can get a copy from London in about three weeks.
If it is the Gessford (New York) picture, tell me and I will
attend to it. I think I like the London one better.*

*The skimming of this house goes steadily on, hour by hour.
There is not an ornament left in my bedroom now but a*

bottle of Scotch whiskey, and somebody has been skimming that.

Paragon of nieces, I herewith enclose my warm regards and respects to Father Fitz Simon; and to you my love.

Uncle Mark

The journey to Redding on June 18 was climaxed by a gala reception waiting Mark Twain at the station there. Crowds of townspeople turned out to greet him in carriages festooned with spring flowers, and they formed a procession which followed his carriage for three miles, to the gate of his hilltop house. The view across the Saugatuck valley charmed him, and the new house, he thought, was perfect in every detail: "I might have been here always." Guests came in that evening, and neighbors set off fireworks at the foot of the garden. The day ended at midnight, inevitably with billiards. Albert Bigelow Paine remembered it as a boisterously happy game.

On July 14 Mark Twain scribbled another note to Mary Rogers, to explain about the picture he had promised her and to express his regret that he could not attend Father Fitz-Simon's wedding:

Innocence at Home
Redding, Connecticut
July 14, 1908
Friday

Dear Lazy: I looked in at Gessford's, and realized that the London picture is much the best; so I wrote to London for it. As I shall be away all summer, I asked that it be sent to Harry, at 26 Broadway. Then, even if he should be in the Yellowstone Park there'll be some one to receive it.

I was told yesterday, in the Grand Central that the other

Rogerses and the Broughtons are gone to Bermuda and have secured houses there. I should have doubted it if it hadn't been told me by a Bermudian.

I have been in this house several hours now, and I like it ever so much.

These—from your very loving

Uncle Mark

I am very very sorry I am not to be with you the 23rd. Do give my love to Father Fitz Simon, and my best good wishes to the bride, if I may take that liberty, on the plea that I know all her people, even if I be a stranger to her.

As a last minute postscript, he scribbled along the side of the envelope:

P.S. The London man writes that he has sent the picture to the office.

He had already sent a letter to Father Fitz-Simon, to congratulate him—"and in the same breath and with the same depth of sincerity," he had written, "I grieve for you. Not for both of you and not for the one that shall go first, but for the one that is fated to be left behind. For that one there is no recompense—for that one no recompense is possible." The new house in Redding reminded him of the house in Florence where Mrs. Clemens had died. It reminded him in a quiet, almost happy way of the comfortable serenity of the large house in Hartford. He liked visitors around him now, particularly young visitors like Marjorie Clinton and Lucia Hull who had come over from Tuxedo Park and who made the house seem alive, as the Hartford house had been. When he heard that Mary Rogers had been ill and was recuperating from an operation, he wrote her later in July, hoping that she also might join them there:

> Innocence at Home
> Redding, Connecticut
> Monday

Why, bless your dear heart, you do give a body such a turn! I was expecting a word from you from the Yellowstone Park these two or three days past—and instead, all of a sudden you appear above my horizon mutilated and in pain! It was very sweet of you to tell me of it first of all your friends, with your own hand. But I wonder you got out of the submerging influence of the ether sufficiently to handle a pencil on the third day. Clara was still torpid and incapable considerably longer than that. I hope to hear you haven't had a backset. If you will come up here I will furnish you plenty of cool weather and the freshest of fresh air to get strong in, and make you very welcome besides. I wish Harry would come, too, but this idea of his of going anywhere on a visit is not merely unthinkable; it's unimaginable! Tuxedo is lovely, but sometimes the weather has spasms of being warmish there.

This house was certainly a very pleasant surprise to me; and I was glad I knew nothing of its shape and character and furnishing and situation until I saw it three and a half weeks ago. It is a home—unquestionably a home. I have lived in only one other house which was able to produce in me the deep feeling implied by that word; that was the Hartford home. I have the New York house for fourteen months longer, but I do not wish to see it again; it was crude and rude, and its too pronounced and quarrelsome colors broke the repose of my spirit and kept me privately cursing and swearing all the time, even Sundays. I am negotiating a return of the property to its owner, after Clara shall have come home in October and consented. It is a good house in many ways, but I don't expect to see it again. This is the place for me, my dear!

I have three neighbors within walking distance—a mile and a half, and I am good for that, after my long tramps up and down Fifth Avenue to show my clothes. Half a dozen other friends live five or six miles from me, and they can easily drive over and see me and lunch with me, and they will do so. And I will lunch with them; but there are to be no dinners on either hand, and no gadding around at night, when I ought to be at home playing billiards. It isn't lonesome here, and I don't intend that it ever shall be. We have two kinds of visitors—week-enders and whole-weekers, for this place is handier to New York than is even Tuxedo. The friends come and go, right along—laps and slams—the new visitor getting into the old visitor's bed before it is cold. One went away this morning; three came last Friday and will remain until next Friday, when Miss Marjorie Clinton will arrive—and Miss Lucia Hull too, I hope, though she hasn't returned a Yes yet, and is probably away from Tuxedo.

We have good times, dear. Sunday services regular. We didn't finish billiards, Saturday night, until three o'clock yesterday morning.

These statistics, these particulars, these informations, unto my dearest niece, along with my love

Uncle Mark

Mark Twain seldom left "Innocence at Home" during that first summer. Near the end of June he journeyed to

Portsmouth, New Hampshire, for the dedication of a memorial to his old friend Thomas Bailey Aldrich. Early in August he rushed to New York in response to news that his nephew, Samuel Moffett, had been drowned in the surf off the New Jersey coast. He made tentative plans to visit the Rogerses at Fairhaven, "but the doctor came up from New York the day before yesterday," he wrote Mrs. Rogers on August 12, "and gave positive orders that I must not stir from here before frost." He resisted and resented illness and age. "I believe I am the wellest man on the planet today," he told Mrs. Rogers. But he did not really believe that, and he was lonely, and every month there seemed to remain fewer old friends to share his loneliness. "I wish Henry Rogers would come here, and I wish you would come with him. . . . I would learn bridge, and entertain you, and rob you." He felt very much like a last leaf, an "oldish relative," he said, when he wrote Mary Rogers on August 17:

> Innocence at Home
> Redding, Connecticut
> August 17, 1908

Where are you at, Mariechen dear? I was in New York on the 4th and 5th—called there by the tragic death of my nephew—and I had half a glimpse of Harry for half a moment—maybe less than that—and so I did not learn how you are getting along. Very satisfactorily, I hope, and that you will drop me a line and say so. Those were a couple of sweltering days, and I got a violent bilious attack out of it after my return home. The hot weather, the heavy black clothes, the depressing funeral, and the spectacle of that crushed and broken-hearted family—altogether it was a ghastly episode.

I had a glimpse also of Will Coe, and extracted a promise from him to bring Mrs. Coe here. They will come in September, by automobile—sixty miles, but they think nothing of the distance. Don't you think you and Harry could do that? I do wish you would. This is a quiet place, on high ground, and you would flourish most wholesomely. And you wouldn't have to play billiards till three in the morning unless you felt that a little dissipation like that would do you good. Our women-guests go to bed at ten or along there, it is only the men that are late birds. We have had twenty-one guests since June 27, and they've all survived. They say they like the place, and I am sure they do. I like it myself; I liked it from the start; and when I was in New York those hot days, I found I had ceased to like No. 21, so I canceled the lease, and now we are fetching its furniture up here; all but enough to furnish a small flat for Clara. Jean goes to Germany early in October, to be placed under a famous specialist in Berlin. And she is glad, for she likes Germany and the language.

Mrs. Rogers writes me from the mountains that Mr. Flagler is there and wants that series of photographs illustrative of the evolution of a moral principle in a person urgently desirous of being good. A Mr. Davies, a friend of his, carried off his series. I remember it. It all comes back to me now. You had a set; and you were to send it to him and I was to have another set made for you. I reckon you forgot it, but it's all right, I will attend to it. At bottom I thought he was joking anyway.

Come—dash me off a line and tell me how you are.

These—from your oldish relative and the one who loves you best—

                    Your uncle,

                                        Mark

In retirement that winter, Mark Twain puttered over his favorite notion that Shakespeare was not Shakespeare, but someone else, probably Lord Bacon, the David Belasco of his time. He wrote long letters to children he had met in Bermuda, and he made new friends among the children of the neighborhood. A Mark Twain Library was established in Redding, and he helped collect funds for it by requiring "every male guest who comes to my house . . . to contribute a dollar or go away without his baggage." The house seemed always filled with visitors: Lord Northcliffe came, and Helen Keller, pianist Ossip Gabrilowitsch, Colonel Harvey, the Robert Colliers, the Martin Littlefields, and other friends from New York. "I've grown young in these months of dissipation here," he wrote Mrs. Rogers. "And I've left off drinking—it isn't necessary now. Society and theology are sufficient for me."

The identity of the Mr. Davies who had carried away Henry Rogers's set of the seven pictures Paine had taken on the veranda at Dublin two years before, so that Rogers could not provide a set for his friend Henry Flagler, seems to have eluded Mark Twain whose memory, even before he reached his seventies, had never been spectacularly good. Though he boasted to Mrs. Rogers that he "was sound as a nut, but nobody believes me," he confessed to a friend in England: "I wish I had energy enough to resume work upon one or two of my several unfinished books—but that is a dream, and won't ever come true." And when he wrote Howells to ask him to bring his family for a visit so that they could all admire his son's architectural triumph, Mark Twain told his old friend: "I have retired from labor for good, I have dismissed my stenographer and entered upon a holiday whose other end is the cemetery." To Henry Rogers he confided,

"I am as brisk and active a young thing as there is in any country—on a brief strain; but it has to be pretty brief."

He wished the Rogerses would visit him also, especially Mary Rogers who had promised but failed to come. His letter to her of March 8, 1909, is on stationery which is headed "Stormfield," not "Innocence at Home" as his former letters from Redding had been, for he had acceded now to Clara's insistence that a more dignified name be given to the new house. The conjunction of the publication of *Captain Stormfield's Visit to Heaven* while the house was being completed and of the discovery by Mark Twain of the ferocity of storms which swept about his Connecticut hillside made the new name seem particularly appropriate.

> Stormfield
> Redding, Connecticut
> March 8, 1909

Mariechen dear, I certainly love you, but that is only because I can't help it; for you are the most vexatious rascal of a niece that helps to inhabit this planet. You are in a class by yourself, and it's well it is so, for there isn't room between the horizons for two of you. Two? It would make chaos, and things would stop going.

I'm well aware that when you say you'll do a thing, you really mean it—at the moment. But that's the end of it. I am like the average person: sometimes I break a promise, but you never keep one. Yes, dear, you are in a class by yourself. I know you are honestly intending to come here, and I know you will gladden me by telling me the day and train; but you know perfectly well that when I go to meet you I shan't find you at the station, and shan't learn why, until I've grown another bunch or two of white hairs. Now I'll wait and see. If

*I am as good a prophet as I always used to was, it will come
out just so.*

*And you did get the picture? I knew it (probably) arrived
last year, because I got the bill for it and for the customs and
duties, but I guessed it had been misdirected, so I blew the
photographer up, and then he blew me up; so he and I stand
even, now, and on the same pleasant terms as ever. I had it
sent direct to No. 26 for some reason or other, instead of to
my house—because I was expecting to be away, I think. It's
a high-art picture—Barnett couldn't make a failure if he tried.*

*I'm going down dentisting and banqueting, March 17, and
shall dine and sleep at H. H.'s, if he hasn't raised the price;
but that I shall have any glimpse of you, dear, is much too
much to expect, for you are the very invisiblest of all the
invisibles. But you can't help that. Land, you're made so!*

You are the hardest lot I know, but I love you all the same.

Your affectionate old ass of an

Uncle Mark

*Next day—which is to-day, the 9th
Letter from H. H., trying hard to say he hasn't any room,
but will refer the matter to Mrs. Rogers. I know what he
means: he is going to raise the price. He thinks I can't help
myself—can't get in elsewhere. But I can: I've already arranged it conditionally.*

*Will you tell Benjamin Miss Lyon and Ashcraft are en-
gaged to be married? I guess it won't astonish him much.*

Miss Lyon was to marry Ralph W. Ashcraft, a young Eng-
lishman whom Mark Twain had employed as a special secretary to accompany him on his trip to Oxford two years before. But the marriage seems not to have turned out to be as

satisfactory as Mark Twain believed all marriages should be. At the time of her death in 1945, the former Miss Lyon was known to her friends, not as Mrs. Ashcraft, but as Mrs. Isabel Lyon.

When business took him occasionally to New York, as it had on March 17, Mark Twain was sure of hospitality at Henry Rogers's mansion on East 78th Street. But, when on May 20 he came to the city again to see Henry Rogers, Clara met him at the Grand Central Station to break the news as gently as she could that his old friend had died the night before. "But there is no way," she discovered, "to break bad news so that it does not carry a brutal shock. The expression of grief on Father's face was pitiful to behold . . . he looked so delicate, enveloped in his shadow of sorrow." Tears ran down his face. "It's terrible, terrible," he told reporters. "I can't say anything; I don't know anything to say." Services were held two days later at the Unitarian Church of the Messiah, at Park Avenue and 34th Street. Mark Twain served with Melville Stone, E. H. Harriman, and William Rockefeller as one of the pallbearers, but he was too stricken to join the funeral cortege to the cemetery at Fairhaven. Henry Rogers's death was a heavy stroke, said Mark Twain: "It bruised many a heart."

Brighter times came that fall, when Clara gave a triumphant concert at Redding on September 21 for the benefit of the Mark Twain Library. Then, a little more than two weeks later, she was married at Stormfield to Ossip Gabrilowitsch. Mark Twain wore his scarlet Oxford gown, Jean was the only bridesmaid, and the Reverend Joseph Twichell, who had officiated at Mark Twain's wedding so many years before, performed the ceremony. "I am glad of this marriage," Mark Twain said, "and Mrs. Clemens always had a warm affection for Gabrilowitsch." The Russian pianist had been a fellow student with Clara under Leschetizky in Vienna. His American debut had been made in Carnegie Hall nine years before, almost exactly a month after the Clemenses had returned in 1900 from their long sojourn abroad. Now the bride and groom, after a brief honeymoon, were to be off to Europe again, to make their home there. The big house at Stormfield promised to be even more lonely.

But then, seven months after Henry Rogers died, Mark Twain's heart was bruised again, and more severely, when on the day before Christmas his youngest daughter Jean was discovered dead after an evening of joyful and expectant preparations for festive celebrations the next day. Her father had returned recently from another visit to Bermuda, for the pain in his chest and his increasing shortness of breath worried his friends. "I can't walk," he had written a few weeks before, "I can't drive, I'm not downstairs much, but I drink barrels of water to keep the pain quiet; I read, and read, and read, and smoke, and smoke, and smoke all the time (as formerly), and it's a contented and comfortable life." But now in his grief, he envied Jean: "I always envy the dead." The last service she had performed for him, on the day before she died, was to send at his request a telegram to the Associated Press in response to an inquiry concerning his health: "I hear the papers say I am dying," he had her write. "The charge is not true. I would not do such a thing at my age."

Mark Twain was not even able to follow Jean's body to Elmira, where she was buried beside her mother and Susy. Instead he sent Edward E. Loomis, who was to become one of the trustees of his estate, and Mrs. Loomis to represent him at the graveside. He busied himself by writing the story

of Jean's life. "It's the end of my autobiography," he told
Paine. "I shall never write any more."

Messages of condolence poured in by the hundreds, more
than he could ever respond to, but their sentiments touched
him. Harry and Mary Rogers's first message was simple and
direct, as it came to him by telegraph on Christmas day:

To S. Clemens
Deeply shocked at the sad news. We send heartfelt sympathy.

Harry and Mary Rogers

Mary also apparently wrote him, a heart-warming letter,
which he answered four days later, on December 29:

Stormfield
Redding, Connecticut
December 29, 1909

You are your old self again, Mary dear, and I am glad. If
you had failed me at this time it would have hurt me—and
you would not wish to do that.

The first letter to come from a friend was from Mrs. Coe;
and the same mail brought six others. I answered them all,
and it took me all day. The evening mail brought some more
from friends, but I was very tired, and gave up trying to
answer them: every mail since has brought others—among
them letters from Mrs. Broughton and Mrs. Benjamin—but
I did not try to answer. Of the letters brought by yesterday's
two mails, sixty-three ought to be specially answered. I am not
equal to it. Of the letters in this morning's mail, twenty-two
ought to have special answers—but I will begin and end
with yours, and content myself with that. I have kept all the

letters from the beginning (many of them from utter strangers, are very beautiful and touching), and shall only answer them with the usual printed card of acknowledgment and thanks. I have read every one of them. Indeed I have done nothing but read letters and telegrams (and annotate and classify them) since mid-afternoon of Christmas Eve. I would specially answer every one of them if I could.

We are in a turmoil yet, and can't take care of a guest, for we are re-arranging things. My secretaries (Mr. Albert Bigelow Paine and wife) and their little daughter have moved into Jean's apartment to-day and vacated their house. They will constitute my family henceforth and be a wholesome change from Miss Lyon and the confederate whom she married to keep him from turning State's evidence against her. I like them greatly—and so will you. Jean liked them.

My other niece (Mrs. Edward Loomis) and her husband, who represented me at Jean's burial, are coming next Monday; Robert Collier and his wife are coming a day or two later (Wednesday) and I hope you can and will come a couple of days later (Saturday). (The train leaves Grand Central—Lexington Avenue side, at 3:32 p.m. and reaches Redding in an hour and forty minutes.)

(Let me know, so I can send a carriage to our station.) I want Mrs. Sybil to come by and by—and Harry; but they would not feel at home in this wrecked and ruined house now. With real love

Your uncle,

Mark

P.S. There is also a good train at 8:50 a.m.

Early in January, 1910, Mark Twain returned for a last visit to Bermuda, to enjoy once more the blue skies there and the brilliant sun, the "picknicking and lazying under the cedars," and the "tranquil contentment all day and every day without a break." But he looked forward to returning to Stormfield when the winter ended, and on February 21 he wrote Mary Rogers, hoping again that she might visit him there or in Bermuda:

Hamilton
February 21, 1910

You dear Mariechen, I've made another botch! and I feel pretty badly about it. When your letter came I put it carefully away with one from Clara which would require about a week's reflection before I could know just how to answer it. Of course I couldn't find them again. Also of course I could not recall the names of those friends of yours whom you had instructed to see me and give me your love. For a few days I was not troubled, for I thought they would get my address at the hotel and call upon me in the private house where I am a guest. But time went on, and I got uneasy: but there wasn't any way to hunt them up. Since I couldn't recall their names.

I never found the letters until yesterday evening, just as I was starting to the Princess Hotel to dine with some friends. I found that the Lees were stopping there, but had already gone in to dinner. I got the head waiter to pilot me to their table—the table of "Mr. and Mrs. Cornelius Lee." It was another failure—it was the wrong Lees. I rejoined my party, and asked the head waiter to try again. He made a search and succeeded, this time, and I asked him to pilot me again. But he said "remain where you are—they are going to speak to you when they leave the dining room." We stayed at the table till the place was emptied, but they did not come. I was obliged to think they were offended because I had not hunted them up when they first arrived. And yet—why? They had not hunted me up, and I was twice as old as both of them put together. I think they ought to have called upon me; and I think it is what you expected they would do. However, they were friends of yours, and this debarred me from standing upon a punctilio—I must not fail in any courtesy that might be due them. So I went to the great lobby and hunted them up. Naturally it was a little embarrassing, but—like the Essex band—I "done my best." I didn't tell them I had forgotten their names, through mislaying your letter; I spared myself that pang. Mariechen, I think they are offended, and will not return my call. But do you think I am any more to blame than they are? I would have sought them earlier if I could have done it.

Would you expect a person to catch a bronchial cold in Bermuda? Well, I have achieved that miracle. A lady brought it from America and I sat at a bridge table with her four days ago and caught it, and carried it to bed and was not on my feet again until I turned out to keep that dinner-engagement yesterday evening. That was my very first game of bridge. It is a bad-luck game. It is not even lucky when you try, out of kindness, to help other people pass the time pleasantly when they are playing it. I have suffered violence for that act of benevolence.

You must pack your bag again, and keep your word, and pay the visit to Stormfield and help me hunt for the garboard stroke when the pleasant weather comes. Only such as are purged of all worldliness can find it, for (necessarily this is confidential) it is really the Holy Grail disguised with a modern name. We can find it, for we are qualified, but no others are, in my opinion. I may not go home until the end of April —then the mystery and miracle of the birth of Spring will begin, and you must be ready.

This is a wonderful June day. Why don't you run down here? I wish you would. Come. You can busily employ yourself out doors all day, with pleasure and profit. (You will note the spelling of that word.)

My health is blemishless except for the pain in my breast. That is permanent, I suppose. It doesn't allow me to work, and it doesn't allow me to walk even so much as a hundred yards; but as it lets me do all the things I want to do, it is not an incumbrance.

With all the love permissible by the statutes.

Affectionately,

S. L. Clemens

Mark Twain returned to Stormfield earlier than he had expected. Friends were alarmed when late in March he reported "having a most uncomfortable time . . . with that breast pain." Dr. Quintard provided Paine with opiates, instructed him how to use a hypodermic, and sent him off to Bermuda to bring Mark Twain home. They left the island on April 12, and two days later Mark Twain was carried from the train to his bedroom at Stormfield. Dr. Quintard and Dr. Halsey were both in attendance. Clara and her husband rushed home from Italy. Four days after her arrival, Mark Twain died, in the late afternoon of April 21. What he found to say to St. Peter about an apartment near to Mary Rogers is not known.

INDEX